Mama Mia Let Me Go!

A journey through the most intriguing lyrics and stories in rock music

An Auralcrave book

Stories for open-minded

They say that music is the art form that most succeeds in triggering emotions, transmitting mood and at the same time communicating a message, often forming a bond between the listener, the musician and the song itself. They also say that music (especially rock) is the medium in which it's most often possible to hide secrets: life stories, elements of fantasy, anything that the authors have inside themselves but that was perhaps not always supposed to be expressed. The things we care about most are those we want to keep to ourselves, without having the obligation to explain them to a stranger, a critic or a fan.

Every great rock masterpiece has a story to tell. Sometimes that story is true, confirmed, provable. Other times we talk about hypotheses, legends, speculation and rumours. Discovering the truth can be interesting, but the whole spectrum of stories surrounding the masterpieces we love includes stories that are not always 100% verifiable: perspectives that are shrouded in mystery, somewhere between reality and interpretation, yet crucial to the quest to capture the secrets of the most important rock works.

Auralcrave's stories for the open-minded have exactly this purpose: to extend the pleasure of enjoying art with the elements that enrich the experience; a process that goes beyond the strict need to distinguish between the true and the unverified. When we talk about art, and especially when we talk about the art we are in love with, to know if what excites us the most is true or only in our imagination is no longer relevant: art wants to consume us, to take us into a world of its own, where what is true may no longer be relevant, because it is what we see that is the true reality. It is a refuge from the banality of the real world, where the contours are always perfectly defined and the possibility of exploring beneath the surface is denied to us.

Art is our world, and nobody can take it away from us. Music is the dimension in which we want to get lost when we need to escape the real world, and the last thing we need is someone reminding us that what we perceive in this or that masterpiece is a simple subjective interpretation.

Many of the stories that you will read in this book are true and confirmed by the protagonists themselves. Others lack this irrefutable proof. We won't tell you which ones belong to one category and which to the other: we suggest you just leave this detail out for a moment and enjoy the journey. It is a journey through the stories and the meanings of the rock masterpieces you love most, a journey where what matters is what excites us, and nothing else. That's Auralcrave's spirit, and there is nothing better when appreciating art.

The stories in this book are written by the following authors of Auralcrave's team: Carlo Affatigato, Ilaria Arghenini, Micael Dellecaccie, Luca Divelti, Fabiana Falanga, Federico Francesco Falco, Dario Giardi, Diego Terzano, with editing from Simon Richardson.

Follow Auralcrave stories on auralcrave.com

Led Zeppelin's Stairway to Heaven: a pathway to human betterment

By Dario Giardi

There are songs that, once you've listened to them, fade away without having any impact. Then, there are others **that transcend music, achieving poetic status and enduring for eternity**. *Stairway to Heaven,* Led Zeppelin's immortal masterpiece, is the latter.

Its lyrics are **rich with cryptic references to allegories and mysticism**, offering far more than the simplistic satanism that many detractors argue is its main theme. Robert Plant wrote the lyrics of course, and he has repeatedly said that he drew inspiration from the works of the Scottish writer Lewis Spence, notably from his book *Magic Arts in Celtic Britain*. And it is that Celtic esotericism and spirituality that truly comes through in the lyrics – no more, no less.

The narrative begins with one of the most famous arpeggios in the history of music:

There's a lady who's sure
All that glitters is gold
And she's buying a
Stairway to Heaven

Who is this ambiguous female figure? Fans of occultist theories have argued that this is a metaphor for an initiation into a new type of Pagan religion; an obscure, unknown belief. But this notion has an easy counter in the many references to Christianity in the song as a whole. According to some, the lady is the Virgin Mary, and Led Zeppelin seem to tacitly confirm this, mentioning the May Queen later in the song, May being traditionally the month dedicated to Mary.

But let's avoid entering into this kind of debate and read the lyrics for what they really represent. When you take the lyrics at face value, you can see that the woman is nothing more than **an allegory of a greedy, materialistic, arrogant society** that believes that everything, including a path to heaven, can be acquired with money alone.

Moving on, Jimmy Page's guitar and John Paul Jones' keyboards embrace us with their ethereal melodies.

There's a feeling I get
When I look to the West
And my spirit is crying for leaving

The West is a clear reference to the idea of purity in the Wild West, which was no longer wild in those days by any means, but is still a representation of adventure, mystery and charm. In essence, it is the place where we can remove ourselves from the materialism of contemporary society and **turn our attention to the unknown, to the stranger**.

Robert Plant wanted to guide us on a sort of spiritual journey, to help improve ourselves and the people around us. And those who hesitate and are watchful (*"Those who stand looking"*), could be those with a conservative outlook, who disapprove of this kind of spiritual journey because they are imprisoned in societal materialism, unable to look forward. But, just when we least expect it, **we will be called to live in peace and harmony**, at one with nature and each other (*"And it's whispered that soon, If we all call the tune / Then the piper will lead us to reason"*).

It is now that we arrive at the famous verse which, if listened in to reverse, supposedly contains a disturbing invocation of Satan. Instead of giving this notion any more airtime though, let's leave the rebuttal to Plant himself: *"To me it's very sad, because 'Stairway to Heaven' was written with every best intention, and as far as reversing tapes and putting messages on the end, that's not my idea of making music."* This really should be enough to put the idea to bed once and for all.

If there's a bustle in your hedgerow
Don't be alarmed now
It's just a spring-clean for the May Queen

This is the reference to May Queen that we mentioned earlier. The bustle in the hedgerow represents our mind, confused by the possibility of this spiritual path, or perhaps simply unprepared for it. But if it's true that you can find many ways to change yourself, then it is also true that **you always have the opportunity to change your mind and take another path**. There are no destinies that have already been written; we are all free to make our decisions with full autonomy.

Moving forward with the lyrics, we arrive at the last verse before the iconic Jimmy Page solo:

Your head is humming and it won't go
In case you don't know
The piper's calling you to join him

It is here when we finally get the call. Our minds are still confused, but the sweet melody of the piper is resounding in our heads, leading us towards spiritual perfection. The message is then addressed to the lady mentioned at the beginning of the song: **the winds are changing and it's time that everyone realises** that humanity can really aspire to something better. At the bottom, the rough stairway to heaven, made of something tangible, is nevertheless floating in the air (*"your stairway lies on the whispering wind"*). It's a path, but it's fragile like any other - perhaps even more so, because it represents the spiritual, not the physical.

The lyrics then give way to Jimmy Page's magnificent guitar, which unleashes a riff, powerful yet dreamy at the same time. It is considered by many **the most beautiful solo of all time**, but it isn't the last word; the song still has something to say in the form of one last appeal to listeners:

And if you listen very hard
The tune will come to you at last
When all are one and one is all
To be a rock and not to roll

The last verse is a synthesis of the message contained in the lyrics as a whole: no matter how great our faults or our dark sides are, we will always have the chance to listen to and understand both those around us and ourselves. **Materialism and individualism will be always present**, ready to tempt us, presenting their way as the simplest and easiest one to follow, but the choice relies on us andour intentions to unite mankind. This is the only way to find harmony, to be united and *"not to roll"*, overwhelmed by a life imposed by stereotypes.

Here it is, therefore, our stairway to heaven: our goal in life, according to Led Zeppelin, must be to discover the power of the community, the need to live together, in harmony with our souls and with nature. Only in this way can we we really improve ourselves and others, escaping the real evil of society, framed in its materialism, selfishness and disinterest towards others (*"When all are one and one is all / To be a rock and not to roll"*).

Stairway to Heaven, in conclusion, is everything but a perverse ode to evil and darkness. In fact, it's quite the opposite, **a splendid message of solidarity, brotherhood and equality**. Together, we can really change the world around us. *To be a rock and not to roll.* Maybe it's just an illusion. Perhaps we will never be able to really get together and do something concrete to make our lives better. But the message is there, and that's what Led Zeppelin wanted from us.

Lyrics

There's a lady who's sure
All that glitters is gold
And she's buying a stairway to heaven
When she gets there she knows
If the stores are all closed
With a word she can get what she came for
Oh oh oh oh and she's buying a stairway to heaven

There's a sign on the wall
But she wants to be sure
'Cause you know sometimes words have two meanings
In a tree by the brook
There's a songbird who sings
Sometimes all of our thoughts are misgiving

Ooh, it makes me wonder
Ooh, it makes me wonder

There's a feeling I get
When I look to the west
And my spirit is crying for leaving
In my thoughts I have seen
Rings of smoke through the trees
And the voices of those who standing looking

Ooh, it makes me wonder
Ooh, it really makes me wonder

And it's whispered that soon, if we all call the tune
Then the piper will lead us to reason
And a new day will dawn
For those who stand long
And the forests will echo with laughter

If there's a bustle in your hedgerow
Don't be alarmed now
It's just a spring clean for the May queen
Yes, there are two paths you can go by
But in the long run
There's still time to change the road you're on
And it makes me wonder

Your head is humming and it won't go
In case you don't know
The piper's calling you to join him
Dear lady, can you hear the wind blow
And did you know
Your stairway lies on the whispering wind

And as we wind on down the road
Our shadows taller than our soul
There walks a lady we all know
Who shines white light and wants to show
How everything still turns to gold
And if you listen very hard
The tune will come to you at last

When all are one and one is all
To be a rock and not to roll
And she's buying the stairway to heaven

The Cure's Lullaby: fight the monster that comes for you

By Fabiana Falanga

I spy
Something beginning with 'S'

In an initial atmosphere which is almost inviting, yet quiet, the beat of the song places us in the ordinary; the normal happenings of a normal evening.

However, soon the beat changes. It doesn't sound like Robert Smith's clock anymore. It has been replaced by something more sinister: **the relentless march of a monster, approaching silently**, crossing the border between death and life, trying to reach Smith who is lying in his bed, paralysed. It's trying to eat him.

The singer's voice crawls along an assertive bassline that endures, despite the presence of the monster. It announces the arrival of the danger, a threat endowed with a sinister power - yet it is almost seductive. It is something that keeps you frozen within your bed, helpless. And it's late to turn on the light.

On candy stripe legs the Spiderman comes
Softly through the shadow of the evening sun
Stealing past the windows of the blissfully dead
Looking for the victim shivering in bed

For Robert Smith the monster is an entity which looks like a spider. It has arrived on his candy stripe legs and now Smith has to face it. It's as fast as fear, too fast for us. **It's subtle, it can creep into the cracks that are left open within our minds**. With its thousand legs, it can restrain every limb, from every angle: like a cage, like paralysis.

Be still, be calm, be quiet now, my precious boy
Don't struggle like that or I will only love you more
For it's much too late to get away or turn on the light
The Spiderman is having you for dinner tonight

There are many ways in which you can interpret the spider crawling on Robert Smith's bed. It has been said that the song is **a reference to Smith's drug addiction haunting him from the past**. Others prefer to think that the song is about the terrifying lullabies that the father sang him when he was a child.

But within the album, *Disintegration,* there lies the despair of one who's lost, and who has no strength to stop the descent. The monster is there. It is fighting us. It is singing to us.

Disintegration is the album that tried to exorcise Robert Smith's state of mind, at a moment when he's completely self-absorbed, at a crossroads in his career. His music, at that time, is trying to break through the armour and bring light to The Cure's true identity. A new birth.

Lullaby is the only song where the impotence of the author is so evident. The horror-like qualities of that album will stay locked in one room: the room where Robert Smith looks the monster in the face, as it tries to make him its dinner. But he manages to lock the monster away.

Because the spider is totally powerless in front of a mind in its full control. Like every animal, it loses against the strength and courage of rationality.

To accept fear means finally facing it, as Smith did that night, in that room. It's an act of bravery.

After that, you can only win.

Lyrics

I spy
Something beginning with 'S'

On candy stripe legs the Spiderman comes
Softly through the shadow of the evening sun
Stealing past the windows of the blissfully dead
Looking for the victim shivering in bed
Searching out fear in the gathering gloom
And suddenly a movement in the corner of the room
And there is nothing I can do when I realize with fright
That the Spiderman is having me for dinner tonight

Quietly he laughs and shaking his head
Creeps closer now, closer to the foot of the bed
And softer than shadow and quicker than flies
His arms are all around me and his tongue in my eyes
Be still be calm be quiet now my precious boy
Don't struggle like that or I will only love you more
For it's much too late to get away or turn on the light
The Spiderman is having you for dinner tonight

And I feel like I'm being eaten
By a thousand million shivering furry holes
And I know that in the morning
I will wake up in the shivering cold
And the Spiderman is always hungry

'Come into my parlor,' said the spider to the fly
'I have a little something here'

Space Oddity: when David Bowie accompanied the first men on the Moon

By Luca Divelti

Ground Control to Major Tom
Take your protein pills and put your helmet on
Commencing countdown, engines on (five, four, three)
Check ignition and may God's love be with you

On July 20th, 1969, the Apollo 11 space mission brought man to the surface of the moon for the first time, realising a dream that had endured for centuries and ending the space race between USSR and USA, with the United States declaring themselves the winners. The event received unprecedented media coverage and was followed by televisions around the world, with TV stations scheduling the event so as not to miss a moment of Neil Armstrong, Buzz Aldrin and Michael Collins's mission.

Among those to provide coverage was the BBC, and during the long live broadcast, it chose a song to play that had been released few days earlier (July 11th), which seemed to fit perfectly the occasion: *Space Oddity*. David Bowie wrote the song after becoming fascinated by the vision of Stanley Kubrick's *2001: A Space Odyssey*, which inspired him to tell the story of Major Tom (the first in a long line of The Chameleon Artist's alter egos), **an astronaut who lost touch with Earth and**

drifted off into the infinity of space.

Bowie was always surprised by the BBC's decision: the song described a failed space mission, and Bowie joked that the station manager had probably just read the title and nothing else. In fact, when they noticed, the BBC actually blocked further broadcasts of *Space Oddity* until the US mission had been successfully completed.

At the same time, you might think there was a rational decision behind the release of the song in parallel with the landing on the moon, perhaps forecasting the media overexposure of one of the most important and significant moments in human history. In fact, Tony Visconti, who produced the album on which *Space Oddity* appears, was uncertain about the song's recording and left it to Gus Dudgeon, saying that he didn't like and thought it was too commercial. It was **only when *Space Oddity* became the album's only hit** that the great producer's mind was changed.

This is Major Tom to Ground Control
I'm stepping through the door
And I'm floating in a most peculiar way
And the stars look very different today

In 1980, Bowie released *Ashes to Ashes,* where he revealed that **Major Tom had managed to get back in touch with Earth and was happy**, but Ground Control warned vilified him, dismissing him as a junkie. It was considered by many to be a reference to a younger Bowie and his addiction to drugs following the success he achieved with *Space Oddity*.

The influence of space and sci-fi on Bowie is also clear in other songs, such as *Hallo Spaceboy, Starman, Ziggy Stardust, Life on Mars, Lazarus, Dancing Out in Space* and *Born in a UFO,* as well as in his parallel career as an actor in films like *Labyrinth* and *The Man Who Fell To Earth.* And his son Duncan Jones, who evidently inherited his father's passion for science fiction, found his first success as a director with *Moon,* the story of an astronaut ready to leave the moon after three years. *Space Oddity* was also chosen in 2013 to the first music video made in space, when astronaut Chris Hadfield wielded a guitar and sang the words, "Ground Control To Major Tom".

Space Oddity brought a 22-year-old David Bowie to the public attention for the first time and **he captured the imagination of a country thanks to the fragility of his alter ego**: Major Tom, lost in his solitude and unable to overcome his alienation, surrendering but not desperate, and acutely aware that there are things bigger than the human race, because…

Here am I floating 'round my tin can
Far above the moon
Planet Earth is blue
And there's nothing I can do

Lyrics

Ground Control to Major Tom
Ground Control to Major Tom
Take your protein pills and put your helmet on

Ground Control to Major Tom
Commencing countdown, engines on
Check ignition and may God's love be with you

Ten, Nine, Eight, Seven, Six, Five, Four, Three, Two, One, Lift off

This is Ground Control to Major Tom
You've really made the grade
And the papers want to know whose shirts you wear
Now it's time to leave the capsule if you dare

This is Major Tom to Ground Control
I'm stepping through the door
And I'm floating in a most peculiar way
And the stars look very different today

For here
Am I sitting in a tin can
Far above the world
Planet Earth is blue
And there's nothing I can do

Though I'm past one hundred thousand miles
I'm feeling very still
And I think my spaceship knows which way to go
Tell my wife I love her very much she knows

Ground Control to Major Tom
Your circuit's dead, there's something wrong
Can you hear me, Major Tom?
Can you hear me, Major Tom?
Can you hear me, Major Tom?
Can you...

Here am I floating round my tin can
Far above the Moon
Planet Earth is blue
And there's nothing I can do

Comfortably Numb: Pink Floyd's masterpiece of incommunicability

By Ilaria Arghenini

A request breaks the silence:

Hello
Is there anybody in there?

In this way, almost as a whisper, *Comfortably Numb* begins: a wonderful poem about loneliness and the need for meanings.

Comfortably Numb, one of Pink Floyd's most beloved songs, from *The Wall* (1979), with its melody and music by David Gilmour and lyrics by Roger Waters, describes a state of loss: the protagonist is **someone who is anaesthetised before coming on stage**.

I hear you're feeling down
Well I can ease your pain
Get you on your feet again

Can you show me where it hurts?

In an interview released in the '80s, Waters said that much of the song comes from something that really happened one evening when, in order to allow him to perform in Philadelphia, the doctor gave him a sedative for a severe stomach ache, which had probably caused by nerves. On the stage, **his hands were numb and his vision blurred, but none of this derailed the crowd**, who continued to dance and sing. And it was out of this that one of the main themes of The Wall came about: the disconnect between the public and the band.

> *"That was the longest two hours of my life, trying to do a show when you can hardly lift your arm."*
>
> Roger Waters

There is no pain, you are receding
A distant ships smoke on the horizon

You are only coming through in waves
Your lips move but I can't hear what you're sayin'

I can't hear what you're saying: there's that distance again, mentioned in the chorus.

You have taken away my pain, you have anaesthetised me, but you haven't made me happy. These are lyrics written with the acute awareness of the melancholy that we experience sometimes, late at night. This song has a very clear vision, carved out of pain and the will to survive.

When I was a child I had a fever
My hands felt just like two balloons
Now I got that feeling once again
I can't explain, you would not understand
This is not how I am

I have become comfortably numb

Incommunicability is a form of pain. Because to be alive, to be human, we need others. We don't need just to be seen, to be perceived: we need to be listened to.

Just a little pinprick
[ping]

Can you stand up?
I do believe it's working, good
That'll keep you going for the show

Come on, it's time to go

Of course, there could be various interpretations of this. In a metaphorical sense, it could mean that **the protagonist has been given a 'fix' in order that he can adequately address his life**, society and relationships, which have become nothing more than a show to him. Society doesn't care about the effects of drugs, just so long as they serve their purpose.

There's no pain, but you're receding. Like a distant ship smoking on the horizon.

As Nicola Randone points out:

> *"In literature, both the water and the sea symbolise our mind, especially the unexplored depths of the unconscious. [...] The complete disorientation of man with respect to his situation makes him feel unable to really express himself and his sensations. That's why the lyrics say: 'I can't explain, you would not understand... This is not how I am'*

The main theme is **the distance between our minds and the perception of reality because of artificial relief**. In other words, we may not suffer, but that does not make us alive; escaping from life and its problems actually deprives us of something. This is the meaning of the song: life is out there; I prefer to face it and let it hurt me, than lose all sense of feeling.

Depression, in *Comfortably Numb,* is just **a grey waiting room, where everything is reminiscent of death**. The absence of pain is not happiness. The doctor in the lyrics takes away the pain to get the show going, but it doesn't work. It only increases the distance, and even the voice on the record sounds more distant.

Our society is based on productivity and success, so reducing our pain or level of humanity to achieve positive results is seen as beneficial. But the risk is that we forget that **the world of feelings, pain, searching, time for ourselves - even fatigue - represents our whole lives**. And it keeps us in touch with reality.

When I was a child
I caught a fleeting glimpse
Out of the corner of my eye
I turned to look but it was gone
I cannot put my finger on it now
The child is grown
The dream is gone

The second guitar solo in *Comfortably Numb* was ranked the fourth most beautiful solo in the history of rock according to Guitar World magazine. The public, however, had a different take on the matter: In 2006, the British radio station Planet Rock asked listeners to vote for the most beautiful solo of all time. Comfortably Numb was the winner.

Lyrics

Hello?
Is there anybody in there?
Just nod if you can hear me
Is there anyone at home?

Come on, now
I hear you're feeling down
Well I can ease your pain
Get you on your feet again

Relax
I'll need some information first
Just the basic facts
Can you show me where it hurts?

There is no pain you are receding
A distant ship's smoke on the horizon
You are the only coming through in waves
Your lips move but I can't hear what you're saying

When I was a child I had a fever
My hands felt just like two balloons
Now I've got that feeling once again
I can't explain you would not understand
This is not how I am

I have become comfortably numb

I have become comfortably numb

Okay
Just a little pinprick
[ping]
There'll be no more
But you may feel a little sick

Can you stand up?
I do believe it's working good
That'll keep you going through the show
Come on it's time to go

There is no pain you are receding
A distant ship's smoke on the horizon
You are the only coming through in waves
Your lips move but I can't hear what you're saying

When I was a child I caught a fleeting glimpse
Out of the corner of my eye
I turned to look but it was gone
I cannot put my finger on it now
The child is grown the dream is gone

I have become comfortably numb

Smells Like Teen Spirit: Kurt Cobain's apathetic revolution

by Dario Giardi

Smells Like Teen Spirit: the manifesto in which Kurt Cobain, Nirvana's lead singer, expresses his anger at a world dominated by greedy businessmen, but also at **the inability of his generation to work towards a viable alternative**. It is a reaction to the seemingly impossible task of starting a revolution within youth.

Cobain himself explained: *"I'm disgusted by my own and my generation's apathy. I'm disgusted at what we allow to go on, by how spineless, lethargic and guilty we are."* This inspired him to paint the picture within *Teen Spirit,* expressed in his own way, through art. Both the lyrics and the video embody his confusion; metaphors, imagery, and symbolism all merge together into his message, for the listener and watcher alike to decrypt. More blatantly, the cheerleaders in the video, dressed in black with the anarchist symbol printed on the uniform, are there at the explicit request of Cobain.

The song became the anthem for Generation X's apathetic youth. **In a world obsessed with success, choosing defeat was a revolutionary act**. People like Kurt, born in the late sixties, had not lived through a World War or fought in Vietnam. The Cold War, cultural repression, divorce, loneliness, unemployment and alienation: that was their Vietnam. Their rebellion was not characterised by epic impulses or idealistic proclamations. It was the ungraceful and spontaneous howl of anger, the moan of anguish. In response to the ethics of profit, to 80s fake optimism, they reacted with sarcasm and apathy. This was their stand: siding with the losers, flaunting indifference in front of catastrophe, and sympathising with failure.

The story narrated through the lyrics begins in the chaos of two twenty-years old's bedroom. An autobiographical event? Maybe... In an interview with Seattle Times, Cobain said, *"We were having a great time talking about revolutionary things, and we ended up destroying my bedroom, the mirrors, the bed, everything that we found. We started to smudge the walls with spray and Kathleen wrote 'Kurt smells Like Teen Spirit'. I took it as a compliment."* The phrase comes from a perfume for teenagers that was very popular at the time, and Kathleen wanted to ridicule Kurt, insinuating that he was not a man yet. Kurt, who was either unaware of ignored the existence of the perfume, instead took the comment as a form of appreciation, as if he had not yet ben subjugated by adulthood, and he still embodied the adolescent spirit.

When interviewed in other contexts, Cobain turned out to be intolerant to the idea of deepening the meaning of the song: *"Basically it's a song about friends, about peers. We still feel like teenagers because we don't want to follow adults. We go around, we try to have fun. The heart of the song is about making a mockery of the idea of putting a revolution in place. But it is still a good idea."* Cobain would eventually plunder his personal diaries to feed the lyrics. **The result is a rabid outburst, a fist to the sky**, so intense that anyone who listens to it, even without knowing what "Teen Spirit" means, has the clear sensation that the song wants to say something, something really intense.

Load up on guns, bring your friends
It's fun to lose and to pretend
She's over bored, self-assured
Oh No, I know a dirty word

The call to arms in the first verse alludes to the revolutionary urgency of a hypothetical youth movement. The opening *("Load up on guns, bring your friends"*), is lyrically powerful and evocative. Michael Azerrad, Nirvana's official biographer, claims that the bored, self-confident girl in the lyrics is Tobi Vail, who was at the time involved in a complicated relationship with Cobain. Vail, Bikini Kill's drummer, was one of the protagonists of the "Riot Girl" scene, a rock reissue of American feminism in the mid-seventies. It was a new protest, this time through music, and one that was firmly against the patriarchal structure of society, the chauvinism and the machismo, but was still not complete enough to elaborate a consistent political criticism.

The frustrated ambitions of the movement were taken as a paradigm of generation X's inability to rise *("It's fun to lose and to pretend"*), a failure that Cobain even recognises within himself. The revolution pursued during the 80s and 90s was, in fact, **a platonic revolution, an inert movement, a paralysis of intent**, a cerebral subversion castrated by the scepticism that had pervaded an entire generation of youth. It is almost a joke, he observes, before returning to what American sociologists defined as *slackness*. In such a situation, it's actually fun *"to lose and to pretend."*

I'm worse at what I do best
And for this gift I feel blessed
Our little group has always been
And always will until the end

This adolescent inadequacy *("I'm worse at what I do best"*) is a constant of post-war American literature. Cobain is the last of that tribe of outsiders, those disaffected young people, **literary rebels struggling with their flow of consciousness**. From here onwards, the song reveals its rabid and helpless nature by ending each verse with a message of surrender: *"Nevermind"*, *"I feel stupid"* (depression), *"a denial"*.

And I forget just why I taste
Oh Yes, I guess it makes me smile
I found it hard, it was hard to find
Oh well, whatever, nevermind

Hello, hello, hello, how low?

Cobain's diaries contain a sentence that Cobain does not use in the final version of the song; a sentence that confirms how self-destructive tendencies can reach extreme consequences: *"The finest day I've ever had was when tomorrow never came"*.

The refrain moves the action on to the stage and highlights one of Cobain's great obsessions - the relationship with the audience and the management of a celebrity that was growing exponentially. This was ultimately a theme that would return tragically in other lyrics afterwards, and in his farewell letter to the world.

With the lights out it's less dangerous
Here we are now, entertain us
I feel stupid and contagious
Here we are now, entertain us
A mulatto
An albino
A mosquito
My Libido
Yay

A denial

In three verses, Cobain moves the narrative perspective from the stage to the audience and then to the stage again. The darkness of the room (*"With the lights out"*) is a mask that temporarily hides (*"it's less dangerous"*) the conscious, contagious stupidity of the entertainer (*"I feel stupid and contagious"*), while the audience calls for entertainment (*"Here we are now, entertain us"*). **It is the psychological drama of grunge's "Fool"**, Cobain, the artist who is conscious of the separation between man and artistic mask; a constraint in which he lives as a prisoner (it is no coincidence that a variation on the diaries says *"segregate us"* instead of *"entertain us"*).

When Kurt wrote his last letter, he was 27. Twenty-seven years old; a beloved wife, a daughter, and yet he addressed his last letter to Boddah, the imaginary friend (the only one able to stay with him through even the most difficult moments) who had filled his solitary childhood, living as an only child with divorced parents. In his farewell message, he revealed that he was no longer able to experience any emotion or to love humans, so much that he felt "bloody sad".

It happens to overly sensitive spirits that they reach such high feelings of love that they finally become unsustainable. Kurt tried to free himself from all the suffering, from all the fear and from the paranoia, immersing himself completely in the music that he saw as his personal "Nirvana" (the term comes from Sanskrit and means "cessation of breath or freedom from desire"). It is a state in which a man can free himself from suffering and problems. But it is a paradise that will turn, however, into hell. From his farewell letter, the second-last sentence is often mentioned, where Cobain quotes a verse of the Neil Young song, *My My, hey hey (out of the Blue)*: *"It's better to burn out than to fade away"*. The last words are particularly beautiful: *peace, love, EMPATHY* – the last one was underlined and in upper case.

The rifle shot with which he decided to end his torments did not only take away only the voice, so mangled and heart-breaking, of the albums which were so unforgettable and immortalised in the history of rock. For before he saw no other solution than death, Kurt Cobain was so much more. A cheerful and spontaneous child, irresistible in his enthusiasm, soon weakened by the unfulfillable desire of a united and happy family. He was a complicated teenager, always out of place, harassed by school mates, determined in his plans to escape from a province populated by "idiots, cavemen and lumberjacks". He was also a curious boy, hungry for experience. Through his eyes, the liberating discovery of music was able to make a flame shine, but it was a flame that could never have extinguished slowly. **Burning quickly was the only option. But while it did, it was wonderful and unrepeatable.**

Lyrics

Load up on guns, bring your friends
It's fun to lose and to pretend
She's over-bored and self-assured
Oh no, I know a dirty word

Hello, hello, hello, how low
Hello, hello, hello, how low
Hello, hello, hello, how low
Hello, hello, hello

With the lights out, it's less dangerous
Here we are now, entertain us
I feel stupid and contagious
Here we are now, entertain us
A mulatto, an albino
A mosquito, my libido
Yeah, hey

I'm worse at what I do best
And for this gift I feel blessed
Our little group has always been
And always will until the end

Hello, hello, hello, how low
Hello, hello, hello, how low
Hello, hello, hello, how low
Hello, hello, hello

With the lights out, it's less dangerous
Here we are now, entertain us
I feel stupid and contagious
Here we are now, entertain us
A mulatto, an albino
A mosquito, my libido
Yeah, hey

And I forget just why I taste
Oh yeah, I guess it makes me smile
I found it hard, it's hard to find
Oh well, whatever, never mind

Hello, hello, hello, how low
Hello, hello, hello, how low
Hello, hello, hello, how low
Hello, hello, hello

With the lights out, it's less dangerous
Here we are now, entertain us
I feel stupid and contagious
Here we are now, entertain us
A mulatto, an albino
A mosquito, my libido

A denial, a denial...

The Police's Roxanne: love, torment and the impossible salvation

By Fabiana Falanga

Roxanne is a prostitute.

The singer is in love with her.

He wants to take her off the street and have her for his own.

Roxanne
You don't have to put on the red light
Those days are over
You don't have to sell your body to the night

Roxanne, you don't have to wear that dress tonight – the dress she wears to attract clients. He wants her to know that she doesn't have to be a sex worker anymore.

Roxanne
You don't have to wear that dress tonight
Walk the streets for money
You don't care if it's wrong or if it's right

The message is directed at Roxanne, for her soul to receive protection from those who have been seduced by her body, captured her and kept her. Now, she's his.

Roxanne is a prostitute and **Sting has set this story in a night in Paris**, watching sensual bodies and melancholic eyes. Roxanne is beautiful, seductive, and for this reason Sting composed a tune with a rhythmic, bossa nova base. It's like a samba.

But if we talk about seduction, then we must really think of the tango. And that's what the drummer, Copeland, suggested.

This is her tango. Roxanne's tango.

In the intro, you hear the laughter of some members of The Police, because Sting leaned on the keyboard of the piano, playing random notes by mistake.

That laughter is The Police.

Born out of a meeting between Copeland (the son of a CIA agent and brother of the future manager and another promoter who managed R.E.M., Simple Minds and The Cure) and Sting, who was in London when Copeland went there looking for music. He had just returned from a trip to Beirut, where he learned a lot about percussion. Henry Padovani, the guitarist, arrived later and that was it; The Police were born. And just two years later, Roxanne arrived in their lives.

This is Roxanne's tango, with that 4/4 beat that drives the song so seductively, like Roxanne's own eyes. Listen to the bass, listen to the tango. Let yourself be thrilled by the beat and you will easily think of a woman, beautiful and melancholic, and she will turn her gaze towards you, attracting you irresistibly. **Sting lends his scratchy voice to Roxanne, telling her story of drama and salvation**. It's the voice of someone who cannot resist her seduction, but definitely wants to scream out his feelings. He will save her.

This is a rock tango; a powerful, brave, determined seduction. But it's still rock, and there is something more: there is the torment and the salvation, the depth and the longing which comes to the surface.

This, we hope, is Roxanne's story.

Lyrics

Roxanne
You don't have to put on the red light
Those days are over
You don't have to sell your body to the night

Roxanne
You don't have to wear that dress tonight
Walk the streets for money
You don't care if it's wrong or if it's right

You don't have to put on the red light
You don't have to put on the red light
Oh!

I loved you since I knew ya
I wouldn't talk down to ya
I have to tell you just how I feel
I won't share you with another boy

I know my mind is made up
So put away your make-up
Told you once, I won't tell you again it's a bad way

Roxanne
You don't have to put on the red light
Roxanne
You don't have to put on the red light...

“Reach out and touch faith”: Depeche Mode’s belief manifesto

By Carlo Affatigato

It’s 1989. In the United Kingdom, mysterious advertisements start appearing in the national newspapers: *“Your own personal Jesus”* and a telephone number. If you called the number, you would hear a short excerpt from the upcoming Depeche Mode single that would signal the launch of *Violator*, their best-selling album ever. The video of *Personal Jesus* would go on to be **the one that inaugurated Depeche Mode’s new rock attitude**, paving the way for their domination of the scene in the 90s.

Your own personal Jesus
Someone to hear your prayers
Someone who cares

It would be Depeche Mode’s first colour video, directed by Anton Corbijn. The decisive guitar riff, combined with the aggressive rhythms, were **something completely different from what the band had produced to that point**, and it was an instant hit with audiences. There were many reasons for its success, but one of the key elements that determined the longevity of the song was the lyrics: a provocative message, that you can easily interpret as a hymn to modern materialism, reusable as an argument against traditional religions. In a world where the only things that matter are those which you can see or touch with your hands, everybody is able to identify their own personal Jesus and build their own faith around him.

The first albums produced by Depeche Mode in the 90s represented the peak of their materialistic imagery. Even the other big single from *Violator, Enjoy the Silence,* says clearly that *"All I ever wanted, all that I never needed, is here, in my hands"*, suggesting that there is nothing beyond what our senses perceive. Depeche Mode have never advocated any religious message or any connections to God - this is undeniable. Yet they always had a God, and they talked about Him many times, from the first album to the last, being careful to communicate that **yes, something exists beyond the world that we perceive, and it is something worth fighting and suffering for**: love. In their previous album, *Music for the Masses,* there was a song, *Sacred,* which confessed in a clear and definitive way what their concept of faith was: *"I'm a firm believer / And a warm receiver / This is religion / There's no doubt / I'm one of the devout."*

Love is the guiding light of Depeche Mode, and this clarifies once and for all that their faith in something beyond the physical world. Their imagery is not made just of pure materialism. But if this is the case, why then is this hymn so clear and clean, and the verses so unmistakable in their interpretation?

Reach out and touch faith

The inspiration for the song and the lyrics comes from the book *Elvis and Me,* written by Elvis Presley's ex-wife. As Martin Gore explained:

> *"It's a song about being a Jesus for somebody else, someone to give you hope and care. It's about how Elvis Presley was her man and her mentor and how often that happens in relationships; how everybody's heart is like a god in some way."*

In Depeche Mode's new rock-star setting, therefore, their intention was to present themselves as **those who could give faith, care, answers to those who need something to believe in**. *"Feeling unknown / And you're all alone / Flesh and bone / By the* *telephone / Lift up the receiver / I'll make you a believer."*

Take second best
Put me to the test
Things on your chest
You need to confess
I will deliver
You know I'm a forgiver

This personal concept of faith, according to Depeche Mode, has always gone beyond the tangible, and love has been always in close contact with sex (another recurring topic in Depeche's lyrics). In *Personal Jesus,* and more generally in the messages they put out through their music in the early 90s, the physical side took over temporarily, and they ended up singing **hymns to the world they lived in**. This all changed soon after, however, following the overdose that took Dave Gahan to the brink of death. Depeche Mode then released *Ultra,* the album that began their second life. From that moment, there would never be again a complete, total abandonment, of the physical world. Love would become, if such a thing was possible, an even more salvific ideal; a firm point that prevents us from succumbing to perdition. And Depeche Mode would move a bit closer to God.

Years later, in *Playing The Angel,* the song *Precious* says:

Precious and fragile things
Need special handling
My God what have we done to You?

Perhaps, in the end, salvation from the world has arrived.

Lyrics

Reach out and touch faith

Your own personal Jesus
Someone to hear your prayers
Someone who cares

Your own personal Jesus
Someone to hear your prayers
Someone who's there

Feeling unknown
And you're all alone
Flesh and bone
By the telephone
Lift up the receiver
I'll make you a believer

Take second best
Put me to the test
Things on your chest
You need to confess

I will deliver
You know I'm a forgiver

Reach out and touch faith

Your own personal Jesus
Someone to hear your prayers
Someone who cares

Your own personal Jesus
Someone to hear your prayers
Someone who's there

Feeling unknown
And you're all alone
Flesh and bone
By the telephone
Lift up the receiver
I'll make you a believer
I will deliver
You know I'm a forgiver

Reach out and touch faith
Your own personal Jesus
Reach out and touch faith

Lou Reed's Perfect Day: a poem about the essence of life

By Dario Giardi

Two different Americas. The first represented by The Beach Boys, The Doors, and the dream of the never-ending Californian summer. The America that supported free, easy. As if it's easy to fall in love without consequences... an America represented by those who took drugs, preaching the message that they did so as an act of awareness and spiritual growth, in order to open the doors of perception or to live out shamanic experiences in the desert.

Then, there is another America. **The one depicted by those who told it like it was. With honesty**. A reality that was told without makeup, not afraid to see the dark side in each of us. The weakness, the fragility, the malice and the selfishness.

There was once someone who was not afraid to tell us that love was also suffering, that it was likely you would meet the wrong people and that feelings degenerate because they are not pure - because none of us can be said to be truly pure. There was once someone who was not afraid to declare that, if they took drugs it was out of desperation, alienation, to destroy themselves; nothing to do with spiritual thoughts or guides. That person was Lou Reed. An artist able to explore the dark side of reality, the things that nobody else talked about, or wanted to talk about. **The dark corners of life, the ones that each of us knows**, even though we would prefer not to shine a light on them in order to keep our carefully-crafted appearances intact, and the places and roles that we have in society.

Lou Reed was able to place us all in front of a mirror, in a strong contrast to the hippie rhetoric of peace and free love that raged in California in those years. He was a deeply sensitive artist, who had touched pain with his hand and seen the darkness with his eyes. Reed was afraid of sleep because the darkness and loss of consciousness took him back to the electroshock therapy (a very common therapy back in the days) he had received when he was teenager, that had been administered to "cure" his alleged homosexuality. If you analyse some of his albums, you may come to realise that the sensitivity of his sublime poetry came from the pain.

Perfect Day, the single released in November 1972 from his second album *Transformer,* is simply the "perfect song". The song that everyone would like to receive as a love message. The most beautiful song on the album, and perhaps the most beautiful song by Reed.

You made me forget myself

I thought I was someone else

Someone Good

These are the verses that I most adore of this immortal poem. It's great to think that there is someone in the world who will help you forget who you are and make you feel better. It reminds me of a phrase from Jack Nicholson's beautiful movie *As Good As It Gets,* where at some point, Jack says to Helen Hunt: "*You make me want to be a better man*". The person to whom Lou Reed is talking in the song is Shelley, one of the most important women in his life since adolescence, the woman who inspired some of the most beautiful songs in his first part of the career (including *I'll Be your Mirror*).

Shelley was Lou's first real love story, which lasted for his whole time at high school. A very complex and psychologically intense story. Reed recalled, in some interviews, how beautiful those meetings were; going to get ice cream, going to the zoo together, seeing a movie. All the while he tells us in the lyrics, that **it is wonderful to enjoy the little pleasures in life**, because we won't have a second perfect day, as the sad melody and the cadence of the voice suggest. That day was perfect and had to be perfectly immortalised, forever, in memory and in this song.

The fruits of those moments will continue to be collected for a very long time, as he says in the last verse: *"You're going to reap just what you sow"*. Behind a good harvest there is always hard work – simple, but so difficult to put in place. It's not easy to listen and listen and understand the difficulties, needs and feelings of each other. **It is even more difficult to put aside our selfishness, our ego and our fears**, to give love, then to learn how to receive it. The concept is deep and extensive; all the books in the world would not be enough to fully explain it, yet Reed expressed and synthesised it in a few, unforgettable verses.

Lyrics

Just a perfect day
Drink Sangria in the park
And then later
When it gets dark, we go home

Just a perfect day
Feed animals in the zoo
Then later
A movie, too, and then home

Oh, it's such a perfect day
I'm glad I spent it with you
Oh, such a perfect day
You just keep me hanging on
You just keep me hanging on

Just a perfect day
Problems all left alone
Weekenders on our own
It's such fun

Just a perfect day
You made me forget myself
I thought I was
Someone else, someone good

Oh, it's such a perfect day
I'm glad I spent it with you
Oh, such a perfect day
You just keep me hanging on
You just keep me hanging on

You're going to reap just what you sow

Mike Oldfield's Moonlight Shadow: the pain behind the appearance

By Fabiana Falanga

The last that ever she saw him
Carried away by a moonlight shadow

You probably sang it while driving, most probably with a smile on your face, like me.

Well, you were wrong. We were all wrong.

Moonlight Shadow is a single by Mike Oldfield, the British composer. Born in 1953, his life has taken him through the full musical spectrum, from hard rock to electronic. This single is from the album *Crises*, which was released in 1983.

The song is voiced by the Scottish singer, Maggie Reilly. But before she appeared on the song, Oldfield had asked Enya. It would have been interesting to see her in action on this song.

Maggie, however, is perfect in her interpretation of the two sides to this song, expressing clearly that *Moonlight Shadow* is anything but a cheerful melody to enjoy during a mid-summer bonfire.

The lyrics are about the frozen shock of **a girl who witnesses the death of her own boyfriend**; taken away in the moonlight, shot to death during a fight. And it's on the ascending climax of the song that Maggie gets angry, finally realising that her love is dying. He was shot right there, under the moonlight shadow.

The trees that whisper in the evening
Carried away by a moonlight shadow
Sing a song of sorrow and grieving
Carried away by a moonlight shadow

All she saw was a silhouette of a gun
Far away on the other side
He was shot six times by a man on the run
And she couldn't find how to push through

Only rock can conceal so much mystery and cruelty behind such quiet notes, a delicate voice, and tones that are inviting like summer smash hits, but yet that carry such a tough message: **the helplessness of the violent and unexpected death of her beloved**.

The bass and drums accompany a guitar that finds its own voice in a solo, like it wants to scream out what the voice cannot say, both mediums broken by the events.

Someone said that John Lennon's death, which happened 3 years before, was the inspiration for the lyrics of this song. And it's probably the only way the audience could accept a song like this, so full of pain and powerlessness.

I stay, I pray
See you in heaven far away
I stay, I pray
See you in heaven one day

We can almost see her; the girl, broken by pain and shock, defeated by a death that happened on a joyous night. Helpless.

The moonlight is the context for what is a paradoxical event. And rock is the sound that realises it.

Lyrics

The last that ever she saw him
Carried away by a moonlight shadow
He passed on worried and warning
Carried away by a moonlight shadow
Lost in a riddle that Saturday night
Far away on the other side
He was caught in the middle of a desperate fight
And she couldn't find how to push through

The trees that whisper in the evening
Carried away by a moonlight shadow
Sing a song of sorrow and grieving
Carried away by a moonlight shadow
All she saw was a silhouette of a gun
Far away on the other side
He was shot six times by a man on the run
And she couldn't find how to push through

I stay, I pray
See you in heaven far away
I stay, I pray
See you in heaven one day

Four A.M. in the morning
Carried away by a moonlight shadow
I watched your vision forming
Carried away by a moonlight shadow
Stars roll slowly in a silvery night
Far away on the other side
Will you come to terms with me this night
But she couldn't find how to push through

I stay, I pray
See you in heaven far away
I stay, I pray
See you in heaven one day

Far away on the other side

Caught in the middle of a hundred and five
The night was heavy and the air was alive
But she couldn't find how to push through

Carried away by a moonlight shadow
Carried away by a moonlight shadow
Far away on the other side
But she couldn't find how to push through

You Know I'm No Good: Amy Winehouse and her fear of being loved

By Ilaria Arghenini

Do you remember Amy Winehouse when she was alive? Every day, dozens of virtual bouquets of flowers are placed in the comments under her songs online, the elegies that are periodically published on the Internet cry out their anguish at the fate that stopped a brilliant artist in her tracks. But the eccentric girl herself, her unique, distinct voice; do you remember them?

I listened to this song again recently, quite by chance. The song was released and found popularity in 2007, but I never listened to it with any real attention. Perhaps I had been negatively influenced by the storyline that ultimately led to her premature death. But I clearly didn't realise how relevant it was. *You Know I'm No Good,* waiting for me among my Youtube recommendations, **stands out from the pack with the intensity of its feelings**.

The album from which it comes, *Back to Black,* had launched Amy to huge success, lauded as being among the greatest British musicians. She became the first British artist to win 5 Grammy Awards in one night on February 10th, 2008, when the album won Best Pop Vocal album. With a sale of 3,580,000 copies in the UK alone, it is now the second best-selling album in the country in the 21st century, and the thirteenth ever.

At that time, Amy met Blake Fielder, the man who would marry her, and with whom she was so deeply in love - but who she betrayed. It happened after a long battle with eating disorders and nights ruined by the excesses. "You Know I'm No Good", she writes in the message bottled within the album, which also contains *Rehab,* her well-known refusal to accept treatment for her alcohol addiction.

But we're not here to focus on the story of Amy and her early death. Instead, let's investigate the song that she gave us, an example of beauty and immortal sensibility. "I'm No Good" reflects the betrayal and perhaps even her last alcoholic relapse. "I'm sorry, I'm trying hard", she seems to tell us, "but I told you I am like this." **Everyone wanted a better Amy. Perhaps what she was asking was just to be loved as she was**.

Meet you downstairs in the bar and hurt
Your rolled up sleeves in your skull t-shirt
You say 'What did you do with him today?'
And sniffed me out like I was Tanqueray

A few details are enough to recreate the scene: he meets her to talk about what happened. He tries to keep calm because he doesn't want to get carried away by her latest betrayal. But it's not easy, and he tries to smell her, to check for the smell of another, as if smelling a bottle of gin to check that it's pure. And she knows how he feels.

'Cause you're my fella my guy
Hand me your Stella and fly
By the time I'm out the door
You tear men down like Roger Moore

She doesn't want to show that she is sorry or weaken herself. He acts like James Bond: stolid and collected; and she as a lover who will not apologise for anything. The request for forgiveness emerges only afterwards, but even then, it's not explicit.

I cheated myself
Like I knew I would
I told you I was trouble
You know that I'm no good

"I'm not a good girl, I'm not like you expected me to be": she can't ask for forgiveness, she doesn't say she's sorry. Instead, she tries to reason that the only person she has cheated, is "herself". **She loves him, but she feels that she is the one who has been screwed**.

Upstairs in bed with my ex boy
He's in a place but I can't get joy
Thinking on you in the final throes
This is when my buzzer goes
Run out to meet you, chips and pitta
You say 'when we married'
'cause you're not bitter
'There'll be none of him no more'
I cried for you on the kitchen floor

She's really in love, she writes in the second verse: Yes, she wanted to betray him, but even at the moment of betrayal, she was thinking of him. And without giving any explanation, she runs to meet him.

The very next scene, there they are, chatting and eating (the detail of the chips creates, with very few words, the notion that it's one of their regular conversations). She knows who she wants, and she is grateful that he didn't leave. They are back together; they can leave this incident behind.

The singer-songwriter is wonderful at creating a climax with music and words, and she saves it for the last stanza, making it even more empathetic. She thinks back to her conversations, afraid that he will change his mind, and sad for having disappointed him again.

Sweet reunion Jamaica and Spain
We're like how we were again
I'm in the tub, you on the seat
Lick your lips as I soak my feet
Then you notice little carpet burn
My stomach drop and my guts churn
You shrug and it's the worst
Who truly stuck the knife in first

Jamaica and Spain - smoke and alcohol. She takes a bath he is with her. Everything is fine, but **he sees the tell-tail signs and senses that it has happened again**. As if the temperature has suddenly plunged, the two stop talking. Once again, he says nothing; he doesn't disclose what he thinks. He's as proud as she is, wounded by the deliberate show of indifference. It was all right, but now it's over. Who's hurting who now?

It is a story of pride. It is the stream of consciousness of a girl who keeps her fears locked away and is unable to apologise. But she's asking to be loved. The words we don't say are often the most important; the phrases that are stuck between the heart and the throat, are often the hardest to express.

Even if I can't say what I should, the lyrics seems to say, please understand. Even if I can't apologise, forgive me. I am also the one who pursues you, asking that we stay together; the one who smiles when you make plans for us; the one who is afraid of being better.

Behind a mask that wants to be strong, a request for forgiveness and help is hidden. I betrayed you but I ran to you immediately: don't leave me, help me change. Loving and forgiving is not easy, and it is even more difficult to let yourself be loved and forgiven, because it is difficult to accept such magnanimity. But at the end of the day, what remains is the hope of being rescued and welcomed.

Amy comes back, every time, with a bag of chips or a bottle of beer. She has no words to say; she cried in secret. She lets him take her back, she lets him forgive her. She wants to be helped to change, even if she will then feel indebted afterwards. **Maybe that's what love really is: the feeling of being wrong, accepting that we are not perfect, then starting over again, together.**

Lyrics

Meet you dowstairs in the bar and hurt,
Your rolled up sleeves in your skull t-shirt,
You say 'What did you do with him today?',
And sniffed me out like I was Tanqueray,
'Cause you're my fella my guy,
Hand me your Stella and fly,
By the time I'm out the door,
You tear men down like Roger Moore,

I cheated myself,
Like I knew I would,
I told you I was trouble,
You know that I'm no good,

Upstairs in bed with my ex boy,
He's in a place but I can't get joy,
Thinking on you in the final throes,
This is when my buzzer goes,
Run out to meet you, chips and pitta,
You say 'when we married',
'cause you're not bitter,
'There'll be none of him no more',
I cried for you on the kitchen floor,

I cheated myself,
Like I knew I would,
I told you I was trouble,
You know that I'm no good,

Sweet reunion Jamaica and Spain,
We're like how we were again,
I'm in the tub, you on the seat,
Lick your lips as I soap my feet,
Then you notice like carpet burn,
My stomach drop and my guts churn,
You shrug and it's the worst,
Who truly stuck the knife in first

I cheated myself,
Like I knew I would,
I told you I was trouble,
You know that I'm no good,

I cheated myself
Like I knew I would
I told you I was trouble,
You know that I'm no good.

Radiohead's Paranoid Android: the only place to escape is your imagination

By Dario Giardi

The first time I listened to Radiohead's *Paranoid Android* and I watched the video on MTV, I was overwhelmed. I had the clear sensation that I was witnessing a true masterpiece; one that would change the history of music.

The song has a direct reference to Marvin the Paranoid Android in the sci-fi saga *The Hitchhiker's Guide to the Galaxy*. Marvin is **a robot who is always depressed because the infinite possibilities within his mind are wasted** on repetitive, trivial activities. His sentence is memorable: *"Here I am with a brain the size of a planet and they ask me to pick up a piece of paper."*

The album's name, *OK Computer*, also comes from a sentence said by another character in the saga: Captain Zaphod Beeblebrox, who shouts: *"OK computer, I want full manual control now,"* as he descends into his ship.

Thom Yorke chooses the most intelligent, depressed character in the history of literature, and sees himself within him: **a young boy with sensibilities and complex emotions, who is suffocated by the alienating world around him**. That alienation is the origin of many of his behaviours, like showering in a hat and putting shampoo in his eyes to wash away his tears, as he imagines another world. He tries to fly away from reality: it's his way to fight the world and escape the abyss, where men pollute their souls and sell their bodies.

The only place to escape is within his imagination. The lyric, *"When I am King, you will be first against the wall"* perfectly illustrates the protagonist beginning to fantasise about revenge in a dreamlike reality - the only place where he can exert power. *"Ambition makes you look pretty ugly/ Kicking, squealing Gucci little piggy"*: is his **condemnation of the materialistic lifestyle that forces you to seek success and money at all costs**. It's an accusation levelled at those who behave brutally, losing all aspects of humanity and empathy because they are too focused on futile things (like that Little Piggy, who loses his temper because he has a drink spilt on him - a real incident that Yorke saw in a pub).

On one hand, we see the naïve, simple boy together with his friend. On the other, a corrupt and petty world, one full of people who don't care about anyone. In his imaginary world, the protagonist creates a different, happier reality, to compensate for real life. Then, he keeps escaping to it.

That's why he imagines an angel who comes to rescue him in a helicopter and plays table tennis with him. **As the young man finds peace and salvation in fantasy, the stingy, corrupt politician destroys himself with his own hands**. He will, however, find someone who will give him a second chance.

God love his children, yeah

They will allow him to born again, after having atoned for his sins. This is represented also by the purifying rain, which comes down from the sky to wash away his sins.

Rain down, rain down
Come on rain down on me
From a great height
From a great height, height

Musically speaking, there is plenty of note. The percussion at the beginning of the song was created with a cabasa, an instrument of African origin, similar to the maracas. The harmonies within the song are wonderful. There is the continuous presence of non-diatonic chords and unusual progressions, proving that Radiohead's songs are anything but harmonically obvious. The structure of the song is incredibly complex. Even listening to the lyrics, you realise the sound research and the hard work needed to compose something so articulate and detailed.

Colin Greenwood said: *"On Paranoid Android, what we were into was the idea of a DJ Shadow meets The Beatles thing."* Thom Yorke confirmed that the original idea came from the Beatles. Initially, there were three songs, but drawing inspiration from the Beatles' *Happiness Is A Warm Gun,* they combined them all together.

Today we can say that they succeeded perfectly.

The entire album is a masterpiece, because it transcends time and date. **It anticipates something; and it acknowledges that when we look back, we realise that things chance**. Even in music. And over the years, Radiohead have constantly pursued this idea, in this instance to see where and how their technique would take them, mixing rock with electronic music. Years later, *Kid A* and *Amnesiac* would be released, proving that electronic music was not only something for DJs.

The path that Radiohead took, more than being prophetic, was reassuring. They declared that music would become more digital and the result would not necessarily be plastic. They were right.

Lyrics

Please could you stop the noise
I'm trying to get some rest
From all the unborn chicken voices in my head

What's that?
What's that?

When I am king, you will be first against the wall
With your opinion which is of no consequence at all

What's that?
What's that?

Ambition makes you look pretty ugly
Kicking, squealing Gucci little piggy

You don't remember
You don't remember
Why don't you remember my name?
Off with his head, man
Off with his head, man
Why don't you remember my name?
I guess he does

Rain down, rain down
Come on rain down on me
From a great height
From a great height, height

Rain down, rain down
Come on, rain down on me
From a great height
From a great height

That's it, sir, you're leaving
The crackle of pigskin
The dust and the screaming
The yuppies networking
The panic, the vomit
The panic, the vomit

God loves his children
God loves his children, yeah

Sympathy For The Devil: The Rolling Stones' diabolical samba

By Luca Divelti

I stuck around St. Petersburg
When I saw it was a time for a change
Killed the czar and his ministers
Anastasia screamed in vain

Sympathy For The Devil is a rock samba that invites you to "understand" the Devil. And it's one of the most famous rock songs ever written.

In 1968, The Rolling Stones had to start again, almost from scratch, and in some ways they did. After the album from the previous year, *Their Satanic Majesties Request,* it was necessary to get back on track and return to rock. The album had been in fact a flop and its long gestation had compromised the serenity of the group. For this reason, they felt some urgency to return to the origins. Keith Richards was the most determined to **leave psychedelia behind, freeing the Stones from a genre that they had only joined because it was on trend**. And the first step in their new, old direction was clear with *Jumpin 'Jack Flash,* a single released in March that enthusiastically embraced Richards' blues and riffs again.

Given the difficulties experienced, the Stones also needed a producer who could guide them without upsetting the delicate balance of the group. Jimmy Miller was the right man at the right time and his experience helped him avoid conflict with the Glimmer Twins. Also, because Jagger and Richards, besides having to write the songs, had to deal with the aftermath of Brian Jones' death, they had become less and less involved in the destiny of the band.

Sympathy For The Devil was born within this context, a ballad inspired by Mikhail Bulgakov's *The Master and Margarita.* Jagger had recently read the novel and that led him to write a song that was close to Bob Dylan's new visionary style. The arrangement of the song was not easy, and the Stones tried various techniques, changing their minds during the way, as they used to do while recording in the studio.

Jean-Luc Godard immortalised the group's creative process in his *One Plus One* film, also distributed under the title of *Sympathy For The Devil.* The director followed the development of the studio song in **a rare and precious documentary of the Stones' working methods**. To be honest, Godard's first choice had been the Beatles, who declined the invitation, leading the production company to choose Jagger and his companions.

In the film, the band is shown in something of a disconnect, designed to reflect the difficult and confused political backdrop of 1968. In the film itself, it's easy to see Brian Jones isolated from the rest of the band, who ignored him as they were busy trying to define the sound of the song.

While shooting, an accident occurred due to Godard's lack of attention: some paper that he placed near some of the studio lighting caught fire, causing a blaze at the Olympic Studios. The arrival of the firefighters avoided a premature end to the structure and increased the already poor relationship that the Stones had for Godard.

Please allow me to introduce myself
I'm a man of wealth and taste
I've been around for long, long years
Stole many a man's soul and faith

The song, originally called *The Devil Is My Name*, went from being a sui generis folk to something totally different. After trying everything, Richards and the others seemed to have hit a dead end. Unable to give a final shape to the song, the Stones relied on the guidance of Miller, who completely transformed *Sympathy For The Devil*. Miller took the song to other shores, changing the rhythm into a devilish, wild rock samba.

The intense, almost primitive atmosphere that emerged from *Sympathy For The Devil* rekindled the band's enthusiasm, and also got the job done. The Lucifer of the song narrates all the misfortunes of human history in which he was the protagonist, and **asks for "understanding", otherwise he will damn the souls of those who don't respect him**. He cites The Hundred Years' War, the October Revolution, the trial of Jesus, the Second World War and the death of the Kennedys.

I was 'round when Jesus Christ
Had his moment of doubt and pain
Made damn sure that Pilate
Washed his hands and sealed his fate

As an aside, Jagger originally only cited JFK, but the murder of Robert Kennedy during the recording period, led them to adapt the lyrics on the fly.

Sympathy For The Devil has become an absolute classic and an indispensable piece in the repertoire of The Rolling Stones. Despite not being a hymn to the Devil as many think, the song trapped the band in a web of accusations about Satan worshipping.

Occultism has never been a point of interest for the Stones, who preferred other kinds of entertainment (especially Richards) and loved to provoke through their songs. *Sympathy For The Devil* was intended to be **an analysis of the dark side of humanity; one which allows itself to be too easily swallowed up by the banality of evil, thereby helping it to accomplish the wickedness it craves**.

If you understand the Devil within yourself, maybe you can

deal with him. And if it's the diabolical Glimmer Twins who are pointing this out, maybe there is something truth in the notion.

Pleased to meet you
Hope you guess my name
But what's puzzling you
Is the nature of my game

Lyrics

Please allow me to introduce myself
I'm a man of wealth and taste
I've been around for a long, long year
Stole many a man's soul to waste

And I was 'round when Jesus Christ
Had his moment of doubt and pain
Made damn sure that Pilate
Washed his hands and sealed his fate

Pleased to meet you
Hope you guess my name
But what's puzzling you
Is the nature of my game

I stuck around St. Petersburg
When I saw it was a time for a change
Killed the czar and his ministers
Anastasia screamed in vain

I rode a tank
Held a general's rank
When the blitzkrieg raged
And the bodies stank

Pleased to meet you
Hope you guess my name, oh yeah
Ah, what's puzzling you
Is the nature of my game, oh yeah

I watched with glee
While your kings and queens
Fought for ten decades
For the gods they made

I shouted out
Who killed the Kennedys?
When after all
It was you and me

Let me please introduce myself
I'm a man of wealth and taste
And I laid traps for troubadours
Who get killed before they reached Bombay

Pleased to meet you
Hope you guessed my name, oh yeah
But what's puzzling you
Is the nature of my game, oh yeah, get down, baby

Pleased to meet you
Hope you guessed my name, oh yeah
But what's confusing you
Is just the nature of my game, mm yeah

Just as every cop is a criminal
And all the sinners saints
As heads is tails
Just call me Lucifer
'Cause I'm in need of some restraint

So if you meet me
Have some courtesy
Have some sympathy, and some taste
Use all your well-learned politesse
Or I'll lay your soul to waste, mm yeah

Pleased to meet you
Hope you guessed my name, mm yeah
But what's puzzling you
Is the nature of my game, mm mean it, get down

Oh yeah, get on down
Oh yeah

Tell me baby, what's my name
Tell me honey, can ya guess my name
Tell me baby, what's my name
I tell you one time, you're to blame

Oh, right
What's my name
Tell me, baby, what's my name
Tell me, sweetie, what's my name

Oasis, Stop Crying Your Heart Out: An Encouraging Message for Us All

By Fabiana Falanga

Hold up
Hold on

These are not words. They are like sirens. It's Liam Gallagher addressing you, in the first verses of *Stop Crying Your Heart Out*. He's sending you a warning. He's your friend and it's time to give him your attention.

A few notes come from the understated piano. The words come slowly, because each one requires its own dedicated focus. Liam's voice is pulsating, resonating. Dear friend, listen to me now.

May your smile
Shine on

It's an invitation, a prediction. It's almost magical. The drums come in and the mood changes. It's almost like, my dear friend, we are picturing your smile.

That smile will help you start again.

That smile will appear on your face, as soon as you let Oasis guide you. You just have to learn how to trust them.

That's their strength, by the way: you can trust them. You play them, and immediately you find yourself. You identify yourself in the beauty of their forms. The golden rule that says that **beauty is born from simplicity**, ring true, and is the most sensual form of attraction possible.

And this is the trademark of Oasis, the last soldiers of the *British invasion,* the bishops of Britpop: direct songs, generational dialogue built on effective instrumental bases, and detailed riffs that grip you, making you dream about the Beatles and the canon of British music history.

Stop Crying your Heart Out is just that: a conversation between Oasis and the listeners of the 90s and the 00s. The song was born as a way for Noel Gallagher to support a friend in need. Since then, the song has **become everything we want to hear from those who love us, when all we need is love**.

Just try not to worry
You'll see them some day
Take what you need
And be on your way
And stop crying your heart out

"Dear friend, you will see those stars again," Liam says in the chorus. His voice becomes a form of guidance, like a lighthouse guiding the way to your inner courage.

The drums you hear before the second stanza represent the first step towards a new happiness and the echo from Noel is simply your own renewed, confident reaction, once you are aware that the stars will come out again.

And the stars do indeed come out. Together with Noel's electric guitar that, in the closing riff - **that extraordinarily simple yet perfect riff** - will whisper the notes of change, of a new happiness. It's a message for the whole generation.

Lyrics

Hold up
Hold on
Don't be scared
You'll never change what's been and gone

May your smile
Shine on
Don't be scared
Your destiny may keep you warm

'Cause all of the stars
Are fading away
Just try not to worry
You'll see them some day
Take what you need
And be on your way
And stop crying your heart out

Get up (get up)
Come on (come on)
Why're you scared? (I'm not scared)
You'll never change what's been and gone

'Cause all of the stars
Are fading away
Just try not to worry
You'll see them some day
Take what you need
And be on your way
And stop crying your heart out

'Cause all of the stars
Are fading away
Just try not to worry
You'll see them some day
Take what you need
And be on your way
And stop crying your heart out

We're all of us stars
We're fading away
Just try not to worry
You'll see us some day
Just take what you need
And be on your way
And stop crying your heart out

Stop crying your heart out
Stop crying your heart out

Red Hot Chili Peppers' Under The Bridge: a ballad to fight your own demons

By Federico Francesco Falco

It's the 90s and Red Hot Chili Peppers are a captivating mix of muscles and hedonism, like **George Clinton's Funkadelic caught in a passionate embrace with rock and the Los Angeles hardcore scene**: a devilish groove, punctuated with four flailing bodies hardened by excess and covered in ink.

There is a documentary, *Funky Monks*, which immortalises three months of intense recordings for what would be their coming-of-age album: *Blood Sugar Sex Magik*. The location is The Mansion, a vintage residence with sinister atmospheres and 10 rooms in the heart of Lauren Canyon (California, of course). A true rock n' roll house, it has placed host to the likes of Jimi Hendrix, David Bowie and Mick Jagger. The film alternates between moments of recording, jokes, discussions about the paranormal (something which Slipknot's singer Corey Taylor also mentions in his book, after having also recorded in the same place) and has a musical appeal that we could almost define as spiritual in itself.

There are, however, about four minutes of the footage that seem to almost move away from the rest of the movie. In them, the frontman, Anthony Kiedis, visits a laundry room in the middle of the night. He isn't the usual mix of Henry Rollins and Iggy Pop, instead appearing close-up, his hair unkempt, wearing a thoughtful gaze that is, somewhat concealed by thick-rimmed glasses. It seems as if he wants to take this opportunity to speak privately with the spectator, as if the latter had accompanied him there for a chat. It's in this instant that Anthony starts talking about one of the two singles that will have a huge impact at mainstream level. It is here that he reveals *Under The Bridge*, a delicate petal on the flower, a fragile ballad that has consumed the last five years of the frontman's life. This dependence on the song has not only taken away one of his best friends, the founding guitarist of Red Hot Chili Peppers, Hillel Slovak, but has also snatched away his own dignity. He has plumbed the depths of desperation, **forced to score his latest fix under a suburban bridge controlled by a Mexican gang**, pretending to be the boyfriend his regular dealer's sister.

I don't ever want to feel

Like I did that day

Take me to the place I love

Take me all the way

But the true content of the song is not drugs themselves, or else the eleventh track of *Blood Sugar Sex Magik* would have become yet another piece of the mosaic of degradation and vice that makes up one of the industry's well-worn clichés. In the song, the city is not a mere theatre of events, but the only real confidante and partner of the author. It is a place that reveals itself before the deep solitude that lies in the eyes of the subject, who has alienated himself through his own struggles and is struggling to find any solace beyond what lies before his eyes. **The naked man stands before his metropolis, his only real friend**. The ending is the point where the climax really captures the potential of the song writing, with an almost angelic choir liberating the song and the writer, who can now see further than the bridge, both emotionally and temporally.

Kiedis never revealed the exact location of the bridge When he was asked outright in an interview with *Rolling Stone* in 1992, he intentionally answered vaguely, in order to avoid imitations. Although several articles have since tried to shed light on its whereabouts, with four possible candidates for the bridge being commonly referenced, no one has yet managed to provide a definitive answer. It is likely that Kiedis locked the answer away in a tangle of multiple clues and references, mixing reality and thoughts with a touch of poetry that will keep the mystery alive forever.

Under the bridge downtown
Is were I drew some blood
Under the bridge downtown
I could not get enough
Under the bridge downtown
Forgot about my love
Under the bridge downtown
I gave my life away

But in this story, there is more than one bridge. The second is a metaphorical structure in the form of John Frusciante, a 21-year-old who was catapulted into a band made up of musicians a decade older. John was not only the replacement for Hillel, but the one to find new momentum for the Red Hot sound, increasing the band's appeal without losing its hardcore fans. It was Frusciante, in fact, who extracted the first piece of music from the lyrics of Kiedis, who was initially **sceptical as to whether such an intimate confession could even become a song**. In this song, Frusciante shows that he has an innate gift that few other guitarists have ever had at this level: intuition, empathy, and a natural understanding of the ideas of his bandmates.

In just a short time, the guitarist built the perfect sound for the mood of the song, invoking two of his greatest heroes as he did so: David Bowie and Mark Bolan. He has said that, for the intro, he was inspired by the opening of Andy Warhol, one of *Hunky Dory*'s most lo-fi pieces, while the idea of the suspended note was a tribute to T. Rex' *Rip Off*, from the immortal *Electric Warrior*. This is all revealed in Amsterdam in 2001, during a brief, intimate tour to promote his album, *To Record Only Water For Ten Days*, in between songs and a sip from a bottle. He goes so far as to define the song as plagiarism, but he knows full well that this is not the case: the notes are different and the way they hold together is prodigious. His mother, Gail Haworth Bruno, can be heard in the choir at the end of the song – the hardest part for Kiedis to sing.

Sometimes I feel
Like I don't have a partner
Sometimes I feel
Like my only friend
Is the city I live in
The city of angels
Lonely as I am
Together we cry

There are two versions of *Under the Bridge* video, both shot by the cult director Gus Van Sant, who was also the official photographer during the writing session in The Mansion. The concept reflects many of the points above; in both videos, Anthony ends his performance embracing himself, the silhouettes of the musicians alternate in a deep sense of unity and Frusciante opens and closes the artistic doors of the movie, **standing on a pedestal like a trophy, bearing an elusive soul**.

These images and the music itself were destined to enter into 90s pop culture. There are a great many references to the song, from the parody written by "Weird Al" Yankovic in *Bedrock Anthem*'s video, to Santana's cover with Andy Vargas , and *The Big Bang Theory*'s comic genius.

Today *Under the Bridge* is a classic of its generation, still full of the bittersweet taste of **a song that still haunts the singer with its demons**. The song is not a permanent fixture in today's live performances, often alternating with two other intense (but less famous) ballads of the same period: *Soul to Squeeze* and *I Could Have Lied*. And if you ask a fan to choose their favourite, they might surprise you. But the one thing that they would probably agree on is that the best version of the song took place in 2005 at *ReAct Now: Music & Relief*, a show that brought together many well-known artists to raise funds for the victims of Hurricane Katrina hurricane. The band performs an acoustic version with deeper harmonisations and a pathos that flows through the strings.

"Sometimes, out of really horrible things come really beautiful things", Kiedis can be heard to say. Perhaps he wasn't just referring to the reason they were there.

Lyrics

Sometimes I feel
Like I don't have a partner
Sometimes I feel
Like my only friend
Is the city I live in
The city of angels
Lonely as I am
Together we cry

I drive on her streets
'Cause she's my companion
I walk through her hills
'Cause she knows who I am
She sees my good deeds
And she kisses me windy
I never worry
Now that is a lie

I don't ever want to feel
Like I did that day
Take me to the place I love
Take me all the way
I don't ever want to feel
Like I did that day
Take me to the place I love
Take me all the way (yeah yeah)

It's hard to believe
That there's nobody out there
It's hard to believe
That I'm all alone
At least I have her love
The city she loves me
Lonely as I am
Together we cry

I don't ever want to feel
Like I did that day
Take me to the place I love
Take me all the way
I don't ever want to feel
Like I did that day
Take me to the place I love
Take me all the way (yeah yeah)

Ooh no (no no yeah yeah)
Love me I say yeah yeah

Under the bridge downtown
Is were I drew some blood
Under the bridge downtown
I could not get enough
Under the bridge downtown
Forgot about my love
Under the bridge downtown
I gave my life away (yeah yeah)

Ooh no (no no yeah yeah)
Here I stay yeah yeah
Here I stay

By This River: the maturity of love according to Brian Eno

By Dario Giardi

Here we are
Stuck by this river
You and I
Underneath a sky that's ever falling down, down, down
Ever falling down

Dreaming is a complex journey. Sometimes, however, it can be made easier, especially when you listen to Before And After Science, Brian Eno's album. One of the best works made by the pioneer of "ambient" music, it's also one of our favourite LPs of all time. It is an album where the irresistible power of Phil Collins' percussion and drums, the cavernous throbbing of Percy Jones' fretless bass and the saucy humming of the synth, pass through us, leaving an indelible mark.

By This River, in particular, is always part of the ideal playlist to take with you to a desert island. A rarefied atmosphere, Eno singing in resigned manner, the piano and the keyboards cherished, as if they are working with precious fabric. A composition that is **the yawn of a soul, a meditation, a masterpiece of calm**.

Through the day

As if on an ocean

Waiting here

Always failing to remember why we came, came, came

I wonder why we came

Like every masterpiece, you can give different meanings to the lyrics. I like to think that the "river" is simply a metaphor for love and the "ocean" represents the maturity of the feeling - the point of arrival. At first it scares you; you feel hypnotised, blown away, but then you understand that this confusion is only momentary. **You get lost, then find yourself**. It's a return to a state of origin, because the mouth, where the river seems to disappear in the ocean, is a containment space, an embrace that holds the river, keeping its course straight and true.

The lyrics sweetly narrate the evolution of all love. It is **impetuous and vibrant as the water is at a river's source, then calm, relaxed, like an ocean**. It's a calm that can frighten, because it makes you think that the passion, the motivation, has been lost on the way. But if you look more closely, the ocean is much larger, much more important, and the limits of the river are endless. The home where you can live and enjoy the maturity of your feelings is, in fact, immense.

Lyrics

Here we are
Stuck by this river
You and I
Underneath a sky that's ever falling down, down, down
Ever falling down

Through the day
As if on an ocean
Waiting here
Always failing to remember why we came, came, came
I wonder why we came

You talk to me
As if from a distance
And I reply
With impressions chosen
From another time, time, time
From another time

All My Love: Robert Plant's Cry for His Dead Son

By Micael Dellecaccie

In 1977, during Led Zeppelin's American tour, while the band was in New Orleans waiting to perform at the Superdrome in front of eighty thousand people, Robert Plant received a call from his wife Maureen. She was seriously worried because of a sudden illness that had befallen their young son, Karac. Two hours later, Plant was informed of his son's death.

Should I fall out of love, my fire in the light?
To chase a feather in the wind
Within the glow that weaves a cloak of delight
There moves a thread that has no end

The tour was inevitably interrupted, and **Led Zeppelin fell into in a very difficult period**: Jimmy Page was completely addicted to the heroine, John Bonham had serious problems with alcoholism and Robert Plant had recently lost his son.

It was up to John Paul Jones to take on the role of the leader. Plant began to consider leaving rock and music, perhaps guilty for being so far away from his family at such a terrible moment, but several months later, he decided to not ignore the pain, and to keep the memory of his son fresh. His return to play with Led Zeppelin, to commemorate him, and at the same time to overcome the pain, represent an awareness that **love and life will be the best cure - both for himself and for the band**.

For many hours and days that pass ever soon
The tides have caused the flame to dim
At last the arm is straight, the hand to the loom
Is this to end or just begin?

In October 1978, Led Zeppelin moved to Stockholm, due to their tax exile from the UK, to record their new songs at Abba's Polar Studios. *In Through the Out Door* was recorded in three weeks, with John Paul Jones testing the possibilities and the boundaries of the new Yamaha synth. It was released on August 15th, 1979, and was totally different from Zeppelin's previous work. In the same year, Maureen and Robert had another baby.

The sixth track, *All My Love,* is **a moving, beautiful dedication from Plant to his missing son**. It was recorded in a single session, because it was impossible for him to emotionally repeat the words in another recording. A legendary song; a love song, but not a romantic one; an act of love that Robert Plant wanted to dedicate to his son. In the lyrics of this song, there is the fascinating figure of the Welsh Goddess Arianrhod, who led the souls of dead to her castle located in the Aurora Borealis, in the middle of the sea, off the Welsh coast.

The cup is raised, the toast is made yet again
One voice is clear above the din
Proud Arianne, one word, my will to sustain
For me, the cloth once more to spin, oh

A year later, the story of Led Zeppelin would end with John "Bonzo" Bonham's death, followed by a few brief reunions with his son, Jason Bonham, on the drums. In 2008, following incredible demand for the "Celebration Day" concert at London's O2 arena (over 20 million bookings in about 24 hours), the band was found to have registered the biggest demand for tickets for a single live performance, according to Guinness World Records.

Plant stated in several interviews:

> *"We tried [to reunite] a few times. It always seemed to be done in a hurry and it never worked. That's why the O2 show was done with such intent. We rehearsed loads so that Jason —John's son — felt like he was part of the band and not just some novelty. We all needed it to be that way. But I can't foresee doing it again, because we all have to agree and agree for the right reasons. LED ZEPPELIN was a creative force that you can't just snap your fingers and create. It was a blend of these four master musicians, and each of us were important to the sum total of what the band was."*

On December 2nd, 2012, President Obama gave Led Zeppelin an award for their contribution **"to the cultural life of the American nation and the world"**.

Yours is the cloth, mine is the hand that sews time
His is the force that lies within
Ours is the fire, all the warmth we can find
He is a feather in the wind, oh

All of my love
All of my love
All of my love to you
All of my love
All of my love
All of my love to you, child

Lyrics

Should I fall out of love, my fire in the light
To chase a feather in the wind
Within the glow that weaves a cloak of delight
There moves a thread that has no end

For many hours and days that pass ever soon
The tides have caused the flame to dim
At last the arm is straight, the hand to the loom
Is this to end or just begin?

All of my love, all of my love
All of my love to you, oh

All of my love, all of my love, oh
All of my love to you

The cup is raised, the toast is made yet again
One voice is clear above the din
Proud Arianne one word, my will to sustain
For me, the cloth once more to spin, oh

All of my love, all of my love, oh
All of my love to you

All of my love, all of my love, yes
All of my love to you

Yours is the cloth, mine is the hand that sews time
His is the force that lies within
Ours is the fire, all the warmth we can find
He is a feather in the wind, oh

All of my love, all of my love, oh
All of my love to you

All of my love, ooh yes, all of my love to you now
All of my love, all of my love
All of my love, love, sometimes, sometimes

Sometimes, sometimes, oh love
Hey, hey, hey
Hey, hey, hey
Ooh yeah, it's all my love

All of my love, all of my love, to you now

All of my love, all of my love
All of my love to, to you, you, you, yeah
I get a little bit lonely

The Passenger: Iggy Pop, a stray's life

By Fabiana Falanga

The Passenger is a single from Iggy Pop's album, *Lust for Life,* released in 1977. The song refers to the long journeys of the rock iguana on the Berlin S-Bahn line. The riff is very catchy - simple but brilliant – accompanying you all the way to the chorus, almost like a game, up to that famous *"La la la la la la la la."*

Singin' la-la-la-la-la-la-la-la
La-la-la-la-la-la-la-la
La-la-la-la-la-la-la-la, la-la

It is in the chorus itself that a new figure appears - David Bowie - described by Iggy Pop as a friend and a benefactor. The voice of Bowie, who was the album's producer, is easily recognisable in the choir sections of the song. Bowie cuts a fraternal figure (as a playmate) and a paternal role (besides producing two of Iggy's albums, he also went to meet his parents when Iggy was suffering, to reassure them about the son – they were living in a caravan and Bowie frightened the neighbours with his car and accompanying bodyguards).

In the song, Iggy describes his usual journey by train. He sees the stars come out, and everything is dynamic. **It's a surprising journey, yet still ordinary**. Then, the song moves into Bowie's car.

On an American tour, the two, in addition to being arrested for possession of marijuana, sat on the back seats, listening to cassettes and talking about music. **A relationship, Bowie-Pop, of union and mutual understanding. Like a team.**

And everything was made for you and me
All of it was made for you and me
'Cause it just belongs to you and me
So let's take a ride and see what's mine

Indeed, Iggy says that *The Passenger* was also written while thinking about the journeys the two took together in David's car, towards infinity.

And that chorus, that *"la la la la la la la la,"* says everything about this life, everything about Pop. It is sung lightly but in a decisive way, as this is the real Iggy: a riff of repeated syllables that can mean everything, but that are repeated because this is what he wants - just like with the friendship with Bowie, his long journeys, and that night-time view from behind the glass window of a train. What does he also want? He want to stray, to embrace his excesses, **his nomadic tendencies and his immense sense of freedom**, full and deep, engraved with the feelings he screams out in his music.

As well as his train journey, which is always the same yet always surprising (as the stars come out), Pop grows more and more excessive, but always remains himself.

Iggy Pop's *"la la la la la la la la"* is **the intentional mystery that shows the artist to be a disordered but coherent chaos**. A star of hard rock.

I am the passenger and I ride and I ride
I ride through the city's backsides
I see the stars come out tonight
I see the bright and hollow sky
Over the city's ripped backsides
And everything looks good tonight

Lyrics

I am a passenger
And I ride and I ride
I ride through the city's backside
I see the stars come out of the sky
Yeah, they're bright in a hollow sky
You know it looks so good tonight

I am the passenger
I stay under glass
I look through my window so bright
I see the stars come out tonight
I see the bright and hollow sky
Over the city's ripped-back sky
And everything looks good tonight

Singin' la-la-la-la-la-la-la-la
La-la-la-la-la-la-la-la
La-la-la-la-la-la-la-la, la-la

Get into the car
We'll be the passenger
We'll ride through the city tonight
See the city's ripped backsides
We'll see the bright and hollow sky
We'll see the stars that shine so bright
The sky was made for us tonight

Oh, the passenger
How, how he rides
Oh, the passenger
He rides and he rides
He looks through his window
What does he see?
He sees the silent hollow sky
He see the stars come out tonight
He sees the city's ripped backsides
He sees the winding ocean drive
And everything was made for you and me
All of it was made for you and me
'Cause it just belongs to you and me
So let's take a ride and see what's mine

Singin' la-la-la-la-la-la-la-la
La-la-la-la-la-la-la-la
La-la-la-la-la-la-la-la, la-la

Oh, the passenger
He rides and he rides
He sees things from under glass
He looks through his window's eye
He sees the things he knows are his
He sees the bright and hollow sky
He sees the city asleep at night
He sees the stars are out tonight
And all of it is yours and mine
And all of it is yours and mine
So let's ride and ride and ride and ride

Singin' la-la-la-la-la-la-la-la
La-la-la-la-la-la-la-la
La-la-la-la-la-la-la-la, la-la

Bohemian Rhapsody: the hit nobody (except Queen) believed in

By Luca Divelti

Is this the real life?
Is this just fantasy?

This is six minutes of pure epic-ness, where Queen poured all their geniality and ambition into one song, conquering charts around the world, and writing their name into rock history books: *Bohemian Rhapsody* is a gem that, so many years after its publication, still leaves the listener dazzled by its lustre.

Bohemian Rhapsody is consistently ranked as **one of the most beautiful, inspired, strange and innovative rock songs**: its switch from ballad to opera, then hard rock, up to the final gong, all that made this song alluring and unforgettable like few others had been before it – or since. Also, the innovative video (one of the earliest and most famous in history) helped to raise awareness of *Bohemian Rhapsody*, which was written by Freddie Mercury and recorded during six weeks of intense studio work, with over 180 recorded tracks and a very demanding speech section (which needed seventy hours of work on its own).

Mama, just killed a man
Put a gun against his head
Pulled my trigger, now he's dead
Mama, life had just begun
But now I've gone and thrown it all away

Mama

The Queen frontman wanted to try out a different structure for the band's songs, and received the approval of Brian May, Roger Taylor and John Deacon, who declared themselves enthusiastic about the idea (even though they weren't really sure about how it would end up). Roy Thomas Baker, their producer, was not so easily seduced by Freddie Mercury's idea: *"And here is where we put the opera section"* seemed a little too vague to be able to get a clear idea of what the singer wanted to accomplish, but eventually the determination of the frontman convinced him.

It seems that Mercury had started thinking about *Bohemian Rhapsody* much earlier, back in 1968, when he was a schoolboy and Queen were very much yet to come into existence. **The story told by the lyrics can be interpreted in a number of ways** (the other band members have always referred to it as hermetic and mysterious). Many have wanted to interpret the words of the singer as a confession about his homosexuality; others as a metaphorical interpretation of a relationship that ended badly.

Too late, my time has come
Sends shivers down my spine
Body's aching all the time
Goodbye everybody
I've got to go
Gotta leave you all behind and face the truth

Mama (anyway the wind blows)
I don't want to die
I sometimes wish I'd never been born at all

The successful layering of genres and melodies convinced

Queen to make *Bohemian Rhapsody* the leading single of *A Night At The Opera*, an album that contained other legendary songs such as *You're My Best Friend* and *Love Of My Life* and that, because of the time-consuming work on *Bohemian Rhapsody*, became the most expensive in history.

For EMI, however, the excessive length of the song was a constraint on its publication as a single. The music industry argued that it wouldn't work on the radio and were at least for a shortened version to be made, which certainly (according to them) would find more fortune and more favourable distribution. Even Elton John, approached by the manager of Queen, said to Freddie Mercury that it was too long and strange to go on the radio. In fact, for almost everybody else, **it appeared to be a suicidal commercial strategy**.

Valuable assistance came from British DJ Kenny Everett, a friend of the group, who received Bohemian Rhapsody *"under the table"*, in order to put it on to the airtime schedule. The success of the song convinced EMI to follow the wave and publish it as a single.

The next problem was promotion: Top Of The Pops, the traditional place where artists presented their hits, was waiting for them with open arms, but the difficulty of replicating *Bohemian Rhapsody* live wasn't to be underestimated. For this reason, the Queen made a promotional video of the song, whose success revealed the potential of music videos, which over the next decade would explode on MTV.

Bismillah! We will not let you go

Let him go

Bismillah! We will not let you go

Let me go

Will not let you go

Let me go (never!)

Never let you go

Let me go

Oh mama mia, mama mia

Mama mia let me go

Bohemian Rhapsody has been **the only song so far to become number one in the UK charts on two separate occasions**: the first time in the 70s and (almost twenty years) later in 1992, a few months after Mercury's death. The single that was eventually able to knock *Bohemian Rhapsody* off the top spot in 1975 was ABBA's *Mamma Mia* (ironically, Queen's song has in the lyrics *"Oh Mama mia, Mama mia, Mama mia let me go."*)

Few other songs have become iconic like *Bohemian Rhapsody*. And if you haven't sung it at least once in your life, in your car, like Wayne, Garth and their friends in *Wayne's World*, you can't claim to have fully understood it.

Lyrics

Is this the real life?
Is this just fantasy?
Caught in a landslide
No escape from reality
Open your eyes
Look up to the skies and see
I'm just a poor boy, I need no sympathy
Because I'm easy come, easy go
A little high, little low
Anyway the wind blows, doesn't really matter to me, to me

Mama, just killed a man
Put a gun against his head
Pulled my trigger, now he's dead
Mama, life had just begun
But now I've gone and thrown it all away
Mama, oh oh
Didn't mean to make you cry
If I'm not back again this time tomorrow
Carry on, carry on, as if nothing really matters

Too late, my time has come
Sends shivers down my spine
Body's aching all the time
Goodbye everybody I've got to go
Gotta leave you all behind and face the truth
Mama, oh oh (anyway the wind blows)
I don't want to die
Sometimes wish I'd never been born at all

I see a little silhouetto of a man
Scaramouch, Scaramouch will you do the Fandango
Thunderbolt and lightning very very frightening me
Gallileo, Gallileo, Gallileo, Gallileo, Gallileo, figaro, magnifico

I'm just a poor boy and nobody loves me
He's just a poor boy from a poor family
Spare him his life from this monstrosity
Easy come easy go will you let me go
Bismillah, no we will not let you go, let him go
Bismillah, we will not let you go, let him go
Bismillah, we will not let you go, let me go
(Will not let you go) let me go
(never, never let you go) let me go (never let me go)
Oh oh no, no, no, no, no, no, no
Oh mama mia, mama mia, mama mia let me go
Beelzebub has a devil put aside for me for me for me

So you think you can stop me and spit in my eye
So you think you can love me and leave me to die
Oh baby can't do this to me baby
Just gotta get out just gotta get right outta here

Oh oh oh yeah, oh oh yeah
Nothing really matters
Anyone can see
Nothing really matters
Nothing really matters to me

Anyway the wind blows

What's Going On: when Marvin Gaye opened his eyes to Vietnam

By Dario Giardi

Understanding is the lifeblood of a true masterpiece.

In order to understand the essence of *What's Going On*, the 1971 album from Marvin Gaye, we need to start with a letter; one of the many that Frankie, his younger brother, sent to him. **In it, he tried to describe the dirty war in Vietnam**, in which he found himself involved, by committing his emotions to paper.

Late at night, talking about life and death, soldiers and the government, whites and blacks. About **veterans who returned home just to be called "murderers"** and to discover that their workplace had been devoured by the economic crisis or by prejudice. The Gaye brothers read, talked and cried. How many African Americans had gone to fight? And how many were dead? How many knew what they were doing? And how many of those desperate black men and boys had been able to read?

You see, war is not the answer
For only love can conquer hate

This story had to be told as well as the street clashes, the frustration of the veterans, the "brothers" who rotted their brains with drugs, the social injustice that starved children and the anger that rose from the streets.

"What's going on?" was a popular greeting among African Americans – the equivalent of "How are you?". The question was **the extreme synthesis of Gaye's bewilderment over the destiny of the nation** and the letters from his younger brother.

Mother, mother
Everybody thinks we're wrong
Oh, but who are they to judge us
Simply 'cause our hair is long
Oh, you know we've got to find a way
To bring some understanding here today

What came out came was a velvet cry, in a compassionate recall, between notes that seem to belong to another world, to another dimension; a different world present in the cracks between the white and the black keys of the piano.

It's like we see Gaye as he reads the letters and feels a sense of inferiority for that brave younger brother on the other side of the world, while he... what was he doing? Who was he? **Perhaps a pampered star. A gear of the music industry.**

He sighs "honey" and "baby" in the songs that the producers of Motown (a legendary record label born in Detroit, called "Motor town" after the large number of factories and car workshops there) gave him. Meanwhile, thousands of young people had died in Vietnam. But there wasn't only the external war to consider. Many black men and boys fought injustice daily on the streets of America.

The echoes of all this became too loud to be ignored. **Marvin Gaye realised that he could no longer hide himself behind sweet love songs**. Life was asking him to take a step forward.

This is *how What's Going On* was born: a spiritual album.

That question was the extreme synthesis of Gaye's loss. A look, full of love, towards a humanity in crisis: mothers who absorb the pain of the community, children who die in Vietnam, fathers who are tempted to respond to violence with violence. In the title track, Gaye sings,

Mother, mother
There's too many of you crying
Brother, brother, brother
There's far too many of you dying

Father, father [...]
You know we've got to find a way [...]
To bring some lovin' here today
Don't punish me with brutality
Talk to me, so you can see
Oh, what's going on

They are simple and enlightening words, answering the question *"What's going on?"* through music. It was love for the community, for your neighbour, translated into a defining melody.

Lyrics

Mother, mother
There's too many of you crying
Brother, brother, brother
There's far too many of you dying
You know we've got to find a way
To bring some lovin' here today, eheh

Father, father
We don't need to escalate
You see, war is not the answer
For only love can conquer hate
You know we've got to find a way
To bring some lovin' here today, oh oh oh

Picket lines and picket signs
Don't punish me with brutality
Talk to me, so you can see
Oh, what's going on
What's going on
Yeah, what's going on
Ah, what's going on

In the mean time
Right on, baby
Right on brother
Right on babe

Mother, mother
Everybody thinks we're wrong
Oh, but who are they to judge us
Simply 'cause our hair is long
Oh, you know we've got to find a way
To bring some understanding here today

Picket lines and picket signs
Don't punish me with brutality
C'mon talk to me
So you can see
What's going on
Yeah, what's going on
Tell me what's going on
I'll tell you what's going on

Right on baby
Right on baby

The Verve's Bitter Sweet Symphony: the desperate struggle against apathy

By Ilaria Arghenini

When I heard again The Verve's *Bitter Sweet Symphony*, I was walking towards the train station. It was 8am on a Wednesday and I wasn't yet ready to start the day. I was thinking back to the sad stories that surrounded this song - and the band that created it. The English group no longer exists; it hasn't done since they broke up in 2009.

Bitter Sweet Symphony, the first track off *Urban Hymns*, is their most famous song. It is so well-known, in fact, that it was ranked 382nd in Rolling Stone's 500 best songs of all time. Thanks to a complicated copyright controversy, it's also **the song from which the group hasn't yet earned a penny**. The band had agreed on a license from Decca Records to use a five-note sample from The Rolling Stones' *The Last Time*, performed by the Andrew Oldham Orchestra.

No problems would have arisen if they had not used more than the five agreed notes, and the song had not had an incredible success. But the combination of those two elements led The Rolling Stones to act in order to secure the rights to the song and be named as authors. Of course, they succeeded in doing so.

But let's go back to my Wednesday, which started without

any verve of its won (pun intended). **The song is perfect for a day when you've got off to a bad start**. When Richard Ashcroft introduced the song at Glastonbury 2008, he shouted, *"Life is a struggle, every Monday morning is a struggle!"*

Well I've never prayed
But tonight I'm on my knees, yeah
I need to hear some sounds that
recognize the pain in me, yeah

How many songs with bitter lyrics and low guitar and bass notes do we know? There are probably countless. But then, one day, this came along. Slowly, the symphony of the strings started to accompany my morning. I experienced the metamorphosis of those streets; everything vibrated with **the beauty of the lyrics, hauntingly accompanied by violins to the end**. I thought that it was impossible that everyone else on the street couldn't see it too. How could a mere pair of headphones and my private experience contain such energy?

The strings don't give up for a second; the beauty of that melody insists, trying to dominate the singer's voice. And the more he cries, the louder they play. It's like a duel.

Cause it's a bitter sweet symphony, that's life
Trying to make ends meet
You're a slave to the money then you die
I'll take you down the only road I've ever been down
You know the one that takes you
to the places where all the veins meet, yeah

No, change, I can change
But I'm here in my mold
But I'm a million different people
from one day to the next
I can't change my mold
No, no, no, no, no...

The music grows as Ashcroft walks through an anonymous

crowd, and it rises above this monotonous routine. **Is it really possible, it says, that it all ends here, with a race for money, with those two extremes, life and death, that have no explanation?** The street is used as a symbol for life. I suspect it's the same analogy as used by Green Day in the opening to *Boulevard of Broken Dreams*.

Well I never pray
But tonight I'm on my knees, yeah
I need to hear some sounds that recognize the pain in me, yeah
I let the melody shine, let it cleanse my mind, I feel free now
But the airwaves are clean and there's nobody singing to me now

I need to know that someone feels my pain; I need their mercy, I need to be seen for who I really am. **Loneliness is not being alone, but not feeling loved**. And those who love you are those who are next to you when you suffer; those who are there when you need to be heard.

That's why he's praying - the lyrics as a whole are a prayer. He cannot speak to anyone, but the symphony inside his head must be shared; it cannot and should not remain unresolved.

I can't change. He repeats it continuously, just like the symphony, because it's what his heart feels. He's repeating to himself. When all around us seems to be inconsistent, we return to our internal struggle, to our dissatisfaction. The change starts when we start looking for something more.

I'll take you down the only road I've ever been down
Ever been down

And then the final verse of the song draws the lyrical journey to an end in an enigmatic matter. Speaking of extremes that meet each other: **is pain the thing that triggers change? Is there a path that allows us to purify ourselves?** These notes are us. We don't know who we are or where we want to go, if we don't listen to our hearts.

That's why, more than twenty years later, we still love *Bitter Sweet Symphony*. **If a song goes beyond the surface of our**

being and tells us who we are, it will remain true forever.

Lyrics

Cause it's a bittersweet symphony this life
Trying to make ends meet, you're a slave to the money then you die
I'll take you down the only road I've ever been down
You know the one that takes you
to the places where all the veins meet, yeah

No change, I can't change, I can't change, I can't change
but I'm here in my mold, I am here in my mold
But I'm a million different people from one day to the next
I can't change my mold
No, no, no, no, no, no, no

Well I never pray
But tonight I'm on my knees, yeah
I need to hear some sounds that recognize the pain in me, yeah
I let the melody shine, let it cleanse my mind, I feel free now
But the airwaves are clean and there's nobody singing to me now

No change, I can't change, I can't change, I can't change
But I'm here in my mold, I am here in my mold
And I'm a million different people from one day to the next
I can't change my mold
No, no, no, no, no, no, no

Cause it's a bittersweet symphony this life
Trying to make ends meet, trying to find some money then you die
I'll take you down the only road I've ever been down
You know the one that takes you
to the places where all the veins meet, yeah

No change, I can't change, I can't change, I can't change
But I'm here in my mold, I am here in my mold
But I'm a million different people from one day to the next
I can't change my mold
No, no, no, no, no, no, no

I can't change my mold
No, no, no, no, no, no, no

It justs sex and violence melody and silence
(I'll take you down the only road I've ever been down)

(It's just sex and violence melody and silence)
Been down
(Ever been down)
(Ever been down)

Because The Night: two opposite souls, one rock anthem

By Fabiana Falanga

Because The Night is a rock masterpiece written by Bruce Springsteen at the end of the 70s. But the Boss realised that there was no room for the track on his album (*Darkness in the Edge of Town*), so he decided to pass it on to Patti Smith, who was recording the album Easter in the studio next to his.

The lyrics were adapted by Patti Smith to be **from a more feminine perspective**. The setting is the evening, and Smith is waiting for a telephone call at around 6pm with a man whom, three years later, would become her husband, Fred. He didn't call. During the wait, she wrote that the night belongs to lovers. She gave up at 2am, but then Fred called her.

Have I doubt, baby, when I'm alone
Love is a ring on the telephone
Love is an angel, disguised as lust
Here in our bed 'til the morning comes

Although Smith is a Rock icon and *Because the Night* one of her strongest pieces - perhaps the first song to secure her place among the pantheon of music greats - it is always a special feeling for me to hear a piece sung by the real father of the song. The mood differs in the two versions, but **you can go wherever you want from a single starting point, with a song as a vehicle**.

These two versions are living proof.

Take me now, baby, here as I am
Hold me close, try and understand
Desire is hunger is the fire I breathe
Love is a banquet on which we feed

Patti Smith's version is deeply feminine. The intro is slow and sensual, and she enters with the anger of a strong woman who has already decided, despite of the burden of waiting, that she will forgive Fred, because this is what she wants. The drums that explodes in a roar say just that: **sometimes, the wait is almost unbearable**, but if you're Patti Smith you can turn it onto a gift from God. Those drums, in the way they arrive, can unleash anything.

Fred will call, and that expectation will turn into excitement; deep excitement, sexual excitement.

Springsteen's live version is another story. The drums arrive more sweetly and softly, leaving room for the Boss's voice. When it comes, it's bolder and firmer. There is also more room for a guitar that makes the song more controlled. In Smith's version, the waiting is the protagonist in itself, and the singer fights against it until she wins. In Springsteen's version, he is the driver, in control - he's driving the night.

Smith fights.

Springsteen decides.

The Boss's live performance is one of the most compelling rock performances ever. The depth of his voice is immense. Springsteen's live version is pure rock: **romance and power together, a decision**. It's a rock roar.

Because the night belongs to lovers
Because the night belongs to us

Lyrics

Take me now, baby, here as I am
Pull me close, try and understand
Desire is hunger is the fire I breathe
Love is a banquet on which we feed

Come on now try and understand
The way I feel when I'm in your hands
Take my hand come undercover
They can't hurt you now
Can't hurt you now, can't hurt you now

Because the night belongs to lovers
Because the night belongs to lust
Because the night belongs to lovers
Because the night belongs to us

Have I doubt when I'm alone
Love is a ring, the telephone
Love is an angel disguised as lust
Here in our bed until the morning comes

Come on now try and understand
The way I feel under your command
Take my hand as the sun descends
They can't touch you now
Can't touch you now, can't touch you now

Because the night belongs to lovers
Because the night belongs to lust
Because the night belongs to lovers
Because the night belongs to us

With love we sleep
With doubt the vicious circle
Turn and burns
Without you I cannot live
Forgive, the yearning burning
I believe it's time, too real to feel

So touch me now, touch me now, touch me now

Because the night belongs to lovers
Because the night belongs to lust
Because the night belongs to lovers
Because the night belongs to us

Because tonight there are two lovers
If we believe in the night we trust
Because the night belongs to lovers
Because the night belongs to lust

Because the night
Belongs to lovers
Because the night
Belongs to us

The Sad Story of the Female Voice in The Rolling Stones' Gimme Shelter

By Carlo Affatigato

There are songs whose magic is comprised of small elements, which at the beginning seem marginal but then become their most identifying aspect. And often, behind them there are particular stories that are worth telling. One example is Pink Floyd's *The Great Gig In The Sky*, with the voice of Clare Torry coming out of an apparently failed audition. Of course, it subsequently became one of the most famous vocal performances in the history of rock. Another example is The Rolling Stones' *Gimme Shelter* and that female scream that can be heard in the chorus. It is **a scream that hides a story with tragic implications**.

It was the Autumn of 1969. The Rolling Stones were in a studio in Los Angeles for the recording of *Let It Bleed. Gimme Shelter* had crude lyrics, in some ways desperate, that **spoke about the ugliness of the world and the need for a shelter** in which to hide when you can't take it anymore. The refrain has a cutting line, which many would sing through the years:

Rape, Murder
It's just a shot away

Mick Jagger said: *"When we got to Los Angeles and we were*

mixing it, we thought, 'Well, it'd be great to have a woman come and do the rape/murder verse,' or chorus or whatever you want to call it." The producer Jack Nitzsche began to call some female singer contacts, despite it being quite late at night. **Eventually, a phone rang**. It was that of Merry Clayton, a professional singer with several important collaborations under her belt, including The Supremes and Elvis Presley. She had also been part of Ray Charles' backing singers, the Raelettes. At that hour she was in bed, in her slippers, pregnant and ready to go to sleep. This is her story:

> *Well, I'm at home at almost 12 o'clock at night. And I'm hunkered down in my bed with my husband, very pregnant, and we got a call from a dear friend of mine and producer named Jack Nitzsche. Jack Nitzsche called and said you know, Merry, are you busy? I said No, I'm in bed. He says, 'well, you know, there are some guys in town from England. And they need someone to come and sing a duet with them, but I can't get anybody to do it. Could you come?' At that point my husband took the phone out of my hand and got angry: 'This time of night you're calling Merry to do a session? You know she's pregnant!' But Nitzsche succeeded in bringing my husband on side. In the end he managed to convince me: 'Honey, you know, you really should go and do this date.'*

She stayed in her pyjamas and hair rollers. She put on a coat, went down to the street and found a car waiting for her to take her to the studio. **She didn't even know who The Rolling Stones were**. They made her listen to the song, then asked her to sing the part about rape and murder. They had to convince her; she was not happy to sing those words at first. She was the daughter of a Christian reverend. But, as she recently told the *Queen Latifah Show*, at one point she started thinking about all the bad news that she read in the newspapers every day, and it was as if something took a hold of her. She sang them for the first time. Then she had to sit down because of the weight of the child she was carrying, and she did a second and third take.

The result is isolated in the extract you can easily find on the internet. You can hear the voice breaking, from effort or emotion, and the shouts of satisfaction from The Rolling Stones as they hear it.

The rest is history. It was the most successful performance of her career, and it would become **one of the most popular rock tracks ever**.

But Merry would remember that night in a very different way, for what happened later. **She returned home and had a miscarriage**. Legend has it that being out that night and making such an effort to sing that part had played a decisive role. For a long time, she didn't have the strength to listen to herself in that song, because of the bad memories of what had happened that night. It was as if it were a sacrifice that she could never accept, until she was forced by events and by the people around her.

In 1986, seventeen years later, she told the Los Angeles Times:

> *"That was a dark, dark period for me, but God gave me the strength to overcome it. I turned it around. I took it as life, love and energy and directed it in another direction, so it doesn't really bother me to sing Gimme Shelter now. Life is short as it is, and I can't live on yesterday."*

What we don't know is whether, after that night, she would have accepted the offer to sing once more had she been called in the middle of the night. Most probably not.

Oh, a storm is threat'ning
My very life today
If I don't get some shelter
Oh yeah, I'm gonna fade away

Lyrics

Oh, a storm is threat'ning
My very life today
If I don't get some shelter
Oh yeah, I'm gonna fade away

War, children
It's just a shot away
It's just a shot away
War, children
It's just a shot away
It's just a shot away

Ooh, see the fire is sweepin'
Our very street today
Burns like a red coal carpet
Mad bull lost its way

War, children
It's just a shot away
It's just a shot away

War, children
It's just a shot away
It's just a shot away

Rape, murder!
It's just a shot away
It's just a shot away
Rape, murder yeah!
It's just a shot away
It's just a shot away

Rape, murder!

The floods is threat'ning
My very life today
Gimme, gimme shelter
Or I'm gonna fade away

War, children
It's just a shot away
It's just a shot away
It's just a shot away

I tell you love, sister
It's just a kiss away
It's just a kiss away
It's just a kiss away
It's just a kiss away

Lover, You Should've Come Over: Jeff Buckley's flowers of evil

By Diego Terzano

The nights that I have spent with Jeff Buckley are not few in number. His voice floats so perfectly over his words; it is so immersed in unity. The unity to which I refer is harmony - **the ability to fight the inevitable degradation that time, or life, bring to our lives**. And even though the existence of the artist himself came to an abrupt end, his voice lives on, resonating in harmony.

Lover, You Should've Come Over is a perfect example of this harmony. Among the songs that occupied my nights (or that I occupied?), this has certainly been the most ever-present, all-pervading as it is with its subtle and vast lyrical balance: as if penetrated by a measured grace. **The song draws your attention immediately to the feeling of lacking – of Buckley's acknowledgement of what's missing**. The words reveal all, outlining the image of a evoked lover who's never present.

The unity of love, now dissolved, retracts and leaves room for solitude - a mirror of what has been lost, and ultimately a sense of melancholy. It is perhaps no coincidence that, among his masterpieces (*The Flowers of Evil*, LXVII), Charles Baudelaire painted such dissatisfaction in a king living in a rainy country, where his melancholy wanders: *Je suis comme le roi d'un pays pluvieux…*

Looking out the door

I see the rain fall upon the funeral mourners...

These first words from Buckley could continue those written by Baudelaire, reproducing their emotional strength: the still gaze of those who observe a funeral procession in heavy rain. There is an anxiety in the tone, and the vocal line, as it swells and grows, acknowledges this, and marks it in the flesh. We burn, after all, exactly as Buckley burns for his beloved, waiting in vain for her sweet return.

So I'll wait for you and I'll burn

Will I ever see your sweet return

[...]

Burning in the corner is the only one who dreams he had you with him

This fire flows through art when it's condensed into iconic, poetically structured images. **Buckley is able to perfectly show you the very essence of absence and love**, singing as he does from a position of vanity – it's his own kingdom, his wealth, his own blood – the perfection of a fleeting kiss, physical contact while asleep, and the delight he derives from her laughter.

It's never over, my kingdom for a kiss upon her shoulder

It's never over, all my riches for her smiles when I slept so soft against her

It's never over, all my blood for the sweetness of her laughter

It's never over, she's the tear that hangs inside my soul forever

These fantasies are rightly well-known. **Buckley is a Baudelairian king, who sees his rainy kingdom collapse before the void**. But while he sings that it's never over, he also succeeds in creating art. When his life turns into music and its harmony, the absence of his beloved grows to the point at which it lives forever within the soul of the artist as an eternal tear. This lacking then becomes beautiful music, thereby returning aesthetic perfection to that which has been broken down by time.

But there comes a time when analysis must grind to a halt. Of course, we could also highlight that the contrast between the interior of the room and the rainy exterior is a metaphor for being trapped between adolescence and maturity (*Well I feel too young to hold on / And I'm much too old to break free and run*); or we could observe that the refrain of the song demonstrates a swing between disillusionment and hope (the beloved should've come over, but – perhaps – it's still not too late...). **But the greatness of this song lies in its perfect balance between pain and genius**. It's beautiful, yet simultaneously evil.

Lyrics

Looking out the door
I see the rain fall upon the funeral mourners
Parading in a wake of sad relations
As their shoes fill up with water
Maybe I'm too young
To keep good love from going wrong
But tonight you're on my mind so
You'll never know

Broken down and hungry for your love
With no way to feed it
Where are you tonight?
Child, you know how much I need it.
Too young to hold on
And too old to just break free and run
Sometimes a man gets carried away,
When he feels like he should be having his fun
Much too blind to see the damage he's done
Sometimes a man must awake to find that, really,
He has no one

So I'll wait for you and I'll burn
Will I ever see your sweet return,
Or, will I ever learn?
Lover, you should've come over
'Cause it's not too late.

Lonely is the room the bed is made
The open window lets the rain in
Burning in the corner is the only one
Who dreams he had you with him
My body turns and yearns for a sleep
That won't ever come

It's never over,
My kingdom for a kiss upon her shoulder
It's never over, all my riches for her smiles
When I slept so soft against her
It's never over,
All my blood for the sweetness of her laughter
It's never over,
She is the tear that hangs inside my soul forever
But maybe I'm just too young,
To keep good love from going wrong
Oh lover, you should've come over, yeah yeah yes

I feel too young to hold on
I'm much too old to break free and run
Too deaf, dumb, and blind
To see the damage I've done
Sweet lover, you should've come over
Oh, love I've waited for you
Lover, you should've come over
'Cause it's not too late

Starless (and bible black): King Crimson's darkest night

By Fabiana Falanga

It often happens that, at night, a sky with no stars becomes **our counsellor, our confidante and the master of our restless moods**, when we are troubled by a life that seems to contradict peace.

On those nights, the sky doesn't appear to be a slice of galaxy, of infinity. Quite the opposite; it looks like the gloomy tent canvas of a desolate circus, the scene for life's sarcastic, bitter show.

The melodic opening of King Crimson's *Starless* (from *Red,* their 1974 album) introduces an apparent calm, an atmosphere suspended by the strings, followed by the notes of the Mellotron and a narrating guitar that seems to open the door to a room, as if urging us to look through a window.

Inside, a man is looking at the dark firmament of the night.

And inside, a prog-rock human drama is taking place.

Deep and powerful, Wetton's voice becomes the storyteller of the journey of the titans at night. These are the companion to our thoughts, riding like dark, powerful horses, galloping between what was and what will be. These are the **thoughts that force their presence on that man, locked in that room,**

under a starless sky.

A man who has forgotten the golden sight of a sunset, to which his longing gaze is directed.

Sundown dazzling day
Gold through my eyes
But my eyes turned within
Only see
Starless and bible black

We can see clearly the anxiety of this man. A man who knows that if he grabs a flower, he will then have to watch it wither. A man who knows the enchantment of the night and who doesn't want to surrender to the inevitable physical shutdown that leads to sleep. For it is a sleep that feels more like death.

So, awake, he continues to drown in a dark night without stars, aware that, after this night, he will learn to swim. He will continue to float on the sea of the life and thought that has been brought about by this night.

An old friend appears, with a perverse smile on his face, offering him compassion.

Old friend charity
Cruel twisted smile
And the smile signals emptiness
For me
Starless and bible black

And this is how, sometimes, it seems easier to attribute familiar faces to our temptations, so they appear more difficult to fight. And then, if you end up giving into these temptations, you can easily justify yourself.

Ice blue silver sky
Fades into grey
To a grey hope that oh yearns to be
Starless and bible black

The dreamlike sea carries the sleepless man in *Starless* and he floats when, like a swarm of bees, a blanket of blue ice comes forward and the sky turns silver. But it's just a moment, then the pleasant sky turns grey, the ice becomes a cage and **the insomniac is trapped as the sea fades**, writhing to the rhythm of Fripp's persevering guitar.

And then, King Crimson's plan comes to life. That ascending climax takes off, higher and higher, faster and more impressive; a guitar frenzy that opens up in the middle of Bruford's drums.

That sea where the insomniac floats has become shapeless, contracted and then enlarged by the musical distortion of those prog rock geniuses. It becomes like wax in the hands of King Crimson, a band that was able to change the form of matter, **to give life and physical form to notes, to elevate the spirit**.

Bruford gives life to the creation of percussion. He moves the night, calling the stars out, then he cries, leaving a space for the introduction of the sax. And **it jumps in and makes fun of everyone**, teasing everything that has been said and done so far. It moves up and down, following Wetton's vocal notes before ultimately giving way to the orchestra of the Kings of prog-rock.

This is life, and even the sleepless man of *Starless* understands it. He is **a man who is too deep, who thinks too much, and who cannot surrender to the emptiness of the moment**.

On that night, the man is hit by the charms of life, by the thunder of the drums, and by the strength of the sax. He is struck hard by the controlled awareness, the charm of decadence and by the majesty of the present. That tension that will force him to surrender to a magnificent truth: **on a starless night, you can see the moon much better**.

Lyrics

Sundown dazzling day
Gold through my eyes
But my eyes turned within
Only see
Starless and bible black

Ice blue silver sky
Fades into grey
To a grey hope that oh years to be
Starless and bible black

Old friend charity
Cruel twisted smile
And the smile signals emptiness
For me
Starless and bible black

Great Balls of Fire: the rise and fall of Jerry Lee Lewis

By Luca Divelti

When you are born in Louisiana in the 1930s and you belong to a poor family, you have very few chances for distractions or fun, especially if you are trying to not starve because of the Great Depression. Jerry Lee Lewis lived in Ferryday and since childhood he had been fascinated by the music coming from the radio and the songs he listened to when he snuck into *Haney's Big House,* the place where Delta Blues was officiated as a religion.

But his relationship with spirituality would later on become a problem, such as when a young Jerry Lee was kicked out of the Christian college he attended; the one that was supposed to turn him into a representative of religious music. A fiery version of *My God Is Real* showed **how unorthodox the approach of the blond pianist was in the songs dedicated to the Lord**, and for that reason he was invited by the presidency of the college to switch to other activities, to go beyond sacred songs.

But the call of the music was too strong, and Jerry Lee had a natural talent: **if he couldn't sing for the Lord, then he would do it for the Devil**. What other chance did he have to escape from the deep south and live a better life?

His parents knew it, and for this reason they bet everything on him and his talent, mortgaging the house for a piano and paying for his lessons. And soon, his skills and the nerve that set him apart him from an early age would lead him to the top of the music business – they were sure of it.

He tried to knock on the doors of some record companies in Nashville, but he couldn't leave a mark, nor arouse much interest in auditions. He had to go to Memphis, which at that time **was the capital of the new rampant religion among young people: rock 'n' roll**.

Sam Phillips' Sun Records was the place that Elvis Presley had timidly approached to offer his talent to the world. Lewis, like many of his future colleagues, wanted to do the same, following the footsteps of the King of rock 'n roll.

The money was not much and the trip to Tennessee was too expensive for the sparse finances of his father Elmo, who had been supposed to accompany his son. Lewis did some maths and found out by that selling thirty-three dozen eggs at the market, and adding to that a lot of thrift, he would be able to pay for the journey for the most important occasion of his life.

Both father and son managed to earn that money and suddenly, the way to Memphis looked easier. In 1956, Sun smelled like success and money: Elvis's contract had been sold to RCA for a figure never seen before; money that was immediately reinvested to launch the careers of Johnny Cash, Carl Perkins and Roy Orbison. Jerry Lee Lewis recorded his first song, *Crazy Arms*, under Phillips' right arm Jack Clement and then returned home, waiting for a sign from Memphis. And from his fate.

My troubled mind knows soon to another you'll be wed
And that's why I'm lonely all the time

After a week the phone rang at Lewis' home: on the other end was Sam Phillips, announcing his trip to Ferriday.

This time, the trip wasn't going to be a problem.

Crazy Arms was published in 1957 and sold pretty well, but the song that really consecrated the rising star of rock 'n roll was next one: *Whole Lotta Shakin 'Goin' On*, which showed the wild and rebellious Lewis who, just like Elvis, was **the best product for conveying a white rocker with the style of a black musician**.

Well, I said come on over baby
We got chicken in the barn

Phillips decided to bet everything on **his new, ambitious, reckless artist who had established himself in the charts with his song and had become the rock 'n roll killer**, ready to undermine Presley's reign. But to take the next step, a hit was necessary, and for this they relied on the pen of Otis Blackwell, one of the best authors of the period. He was the one who wrote *Great Balls Of Fire* for Lewis.

I learned to love all of Hollywood money
You came along and you moved me honey
I changed my mind, looking fine
Goodness gracious great balls of fire

Blackwell probably had a great time conceiving the piece, which was based on a vulgar expression that was very much in vogue in the southern United States, and therefore known to the pianist. The "Balls of Fire" of the title was **a little word pun, taking up an idiomatic phrase which had been used to express exasperation, but that was also used to show appreciation for something in a colourful way**. The expression came from biblical passages and had then evolved into an exclamation of amazement. It can be compared to *"Great Scott!"* as used by Doc in *Back to the Future*. Or, more simply, today we would say: *"Cool!"*

Great Balls of Fire told, through the many allusions and ambiguities that were typical of early rock 'n roll songs, **a story of sex between two novice lovers**, aware they were doing something forbidden, but who were unable to stop.

You kissed me baby, woo, it feels good
Hold me baby, learn to let me love you like a lover should
You're fine, so kind
I'm a nervous world that you're mine mine mine mine

The rhythm of the song is composed by just two instruments - the drums and the piano, the latter played by a frightened Lewis, who infuses all his overwhelming and anarchic impetuosity.

Great Balls Of Fire is the manifesto of Lewis' style, who **on the one hand conquered young people with his provocative, rebel sensuality, while on the other disturbing their the parents**, who were terrified by the seductive capacity of this blond Lucifer. And seduction was in fact one of Lewis' distinguishing marks - especially when you consider that at the time of *Great Balls Of Fire*'s release he was already on his third marriage. His new bride was Myra Gale Brown, a 13-year-old distant cousin: something that Phillips and his entourage were very careful to hide from the press, so as not to create unnecessary scandals for the restless Lewis. But in the long run, the story came out.

In 1958, when Lewismania was at its peak and there a profitable tour in England was about to come, the Killer demanded to have the girl next to him on the trip, underestimating the risks. The identity and the age of Myra were discovered by the English press, which massacred Lewis and depicted him as a monster that **not only infested radios with his diabolical songs, but also represented an incestuous corruptor of girls**.

The tour was cancelled, and Lewis departed with his tail between his legs. The scandal of course reached also the United States and ultimately, he had no chance. After only one year as a king, Jerry Lee Lewis had a radiant past behind him, while his future was more uncertain than ever.

Everybody drifted away and no one remained by his side, forcing him into years of darkness. At the end of the sixties, Lewis recycled himself as a country singer and succeeded in getting some satisfaction, but **the regret of the past never abandoned him**.

Jerry Lee Lewis was **a violent, sudden fire that burned everything in a short time and then disappeared**, leaving only floating ash. But as long as it lasted, it was "cool".

I cut my nails and I twiddle my thumbs
I'm really nervous but it sure is fun
Come on baby, you drive me crazy

Lyrics

You shake my nerves and you rattle my brain
Too much love drives a man insane
You broke my will, oh what a thrill
Goodness gracious great balls of fire

I learned to love all of Hollywood money
You came along and you moved me honey
I changed my mind, looking fine
Goodness gracious great balls of fire

You kissed me baby, woo, it feels good
Hold me baby, learn to let me love you like a lover should
You're fine, so kind
I'm a nervous world that your mine mine mine mine

I cut my nails and I twiddle my thumbs
I'm really nervous but it sure is fun
Come on baby, you drive me crazy
Goodness gracious great balls of fire

Well kiss me baby, woo-oooooo, it feels good
Hold me baby
I want to love you like a lover should
You're fine, so kind
I got this world that you're mine mine mine mine

I cut my nails and I twiddle my thumbs
I'm real nervous 'cause it sure is fun
Come on baby, you drive me crazy
Goodness gracious great balls of fire

The Man Who Sold The World: David Bowie and his detachment from reality

By Dario Giardi

The Man Who Sold the World is a song written by David Bowie (although many continue to think that it was by Nirvana) that, after years, still remains enigmatic. The lyrics, which can be interpreted in many ways, and the different perspectives from which you can compare them to Bowie's life and temper, all add to the intrigue.

Oh no, not me
I never lost control

Let's start from this verse. David Bowie wants to highlight a difference between him and someone else, who has in some way lost control. But not him. He says it clearly.

So who lost control? And about what?

The protagonist of the story has lost control over his perception of reality. This individual could be any of us; overwhelmed by frenetic modern times, we hide and transform our beings, our appearances and our thinking.

You're face to face
With the man who sold the world

Whoever has lied to themselves, anyone who has benefited from being mistaken for someone else, whoever has created a character or guise, or a world in which there hasn't been success, can be considered *"the man who sold the world"*.

Losing control with reality, we seriously risk forgetting who we really are. We adapt to the mask that we wear because that's what society wants from us, and we believe that **only by selling our own world, our way of being, could we be accepted**. We think this is the only way to become a part of the society around us.

He said I was his friend
Which came as some surprise
I spoke into his eyes
I thought you died alone
A long long time ago

This is who Bowie is talking about: all the people who, in order to achieve something, **transform their own truth and life and hide behind a mask**, minimising their "ego", like a feeble flame that is being extinguished. But this is like hiding dust under the rug: there is no way to erase what or who we are and that same rug will begin to swell, sooner or later.

Many, however, prefer to ignore this and continue to sell the world to conquer love, to succeed at work, to be always at the top in a community that drives us to be and to do more and more.

I laughed and shook his hand
And made my way back home
I searched for form and land
For years and years I roamed

Perhaps the song was written for himself. Even though, as we have seen in the beginning, Bowie tries in all ways to distance himself from these types of individuals; he wants to emphasise that he is not like everyone else. He perceives within himself **a Bowie who is different from the mask that everyone knows**, different from the rock star. Under the mask that has been created, there is his ego, his world - the real one. In the song, he has an encounter with a part of himself that he's been thinking was dead for years. But luckily, it was still alive.

In 1997, in an interview with BBC, David Bowie revealed:

> *"I think I wrote it because there was a part of me that I was still looking for... For me that song has always exemplified the state of mind that you feel when you are young, when you realise that there is a part of us that we have not yet managed to put together, there is this great research, a great need to really understand who we are."*

I gazed a gazely stare
At all the millions here
We must have died alone
A long long time ago

Lyrics

We passed upon the stair
We spoke of was and when
Although I wasn't there
He said I was his friend
Which came as a surprise
I spoke into his eyes
I thought you died alone
A long long time ago

Oh no, not me
We never lost control
You're face to face
With the man who sold the world

I laughed and shook his hand
And made my way back home
I searched for form and land
For years and years I roamed
I gazed a gazely stare
We walked a million hills
I must have died alone
A long, long time ago

Who knows?
Not me
I never lost control
You're face to face
With the man who sold the world

Who knows?
Not me
We never lost control
You're face to face
With the man who sold the world

Don't Let Me Down: John Lennon's love song for Yoko Ono

By Micael Dellecaccie

The music of the Beatles is timeless and adored all over the world. Their work is the subject of study in universities globally, and the places linked to the history of the Beatles are continuously visited by music pilgrims.

The history of music's most key moments contains a great many references to the band and their songs, which conquered the world. It is a story, however, that ended at a precise date: January 30th, 1969, the day when the Beatles climbed to the fifth floor of the building of the record label they owned, Apple Corps, at 3 Savile Row in London, and began **a concert that lasted for forty-two minutes. It was the famous Rooftop Concert.**

It was the last time Fab Four played live together.

The recordings of *Let It Be* were in progress, and with them, the eponymous docu-film. The traffic stopped and a crowd gathered under the building, until the police arrived, climbed onto the roof and ordered the group to stop playing.

Talking about that concert, Ringo Starr said:

"There was a plan to play live somewhere. We were wondering where we could go – 'Oh, the Palladium or the Sahara'. But we would have had to take all the stuff, so we decided, 'Let's get up on the roof.'"

That day, John Lennon sang a song that had been recorded a couple of days before, during their recording of the single *Get Back*. It was called *Don't Let Me Down* and it was one of the most sincere and touching love songs he ever wrote. That day, for the Rooftop Concert, he sang it with Yoko Ono's gaze on him the whole time.

Don't let me down
Don't let me down
Nobody ever loved me like she does
Oh, she does, yeah, she does

The song is a return to simplicity, both in the lyrics and the music, lacking the psychedelic sounds or sophisticated content that the Beatles had been experimenting with. The lyrics are all about true love and its duration, and in those verses, Lennon manifests the fear that Ono might betray or abandon him. **He appears incredibly fragile and in need of affection, like a man who fears being disappointed by others**. It was a legacy of the bitter moments of his childhood, when, as a child his parents let his aunt Mimi take care of him.

Other versions of this song were recorded; one was included on the 1970 B side of *Hey Jude* and another in the soundtrack of the documentary *Imagine: John Lennon*. But the performance of *Don't Let Me Down* on Apple Corps' roof is still the most memorable version of the song.

Lyrics

Don't let me down
Don't let me down

Nobody ever loved me like she does
Oh, she does, yeah, she does
And if somebody loved me like she do me
Oh, she do me, yes, she does

Don't let me down
Don't let me down

I'm in love for the first time
Don't you know it's gonna last
It's a love that lasts forever
It's a love that had no past

Don't let me down
Don't let me down

And from the first time that she really done me
Oh, she done me, she done me good
I guess nobody ever really done me
Oh, she done me, she done me good

Don't let me down
Don't let me down

Massive Attack's Teardrop: the fragility of love, the delirium of a night

By Fabiana Falanga

If there are any modern lyrics that are able to express the mysticism of a night of rituals, they are definitely found in Massive Attack's *Teardrop,* from their album *Mezzanine,* released in 1998.

It is a song that tells us the story of a woman **on a dark and mysterious night of passionate delirium**, who seeks the truth about love.

And she gets an answer. From Massive Attack, the pioneers of trip hop, a genre that goes beyond any compartmentalisation, refusing to belong or relate to any other music genre. It is an approach that brings new elements to modern music, while taking its inspiration from a large set of predecessors, from jazz, to electronic music, to rock.

Love, love is a verb
Love is a doing word

The start is like a pulse, similar to a heartbeat. It determines the rhythm and where the melodic line jumps in, metallic and enigmatic, followed by those slow notes. It's like a pendulum, a clock that introduces a story to us.

The solemnity is palpable, as if time has stopped for a moment, in order to make room for a concept or an explanation.

Massive Attack are trying to tell us what love is.

Teardrop on fire

The beat of the song perfectly represents **the fragility of such an ethereal concept as love**. It is fragile like the crystal of a teardrop, yet powerful like a droplet falling into a fire.

Love is a doing word. And the song is an act of impulse; the beat comes from our heart and it's just meant to express the feeling: breath, heartbeat, action, then life.

The teardrop is static; the action is in the beat.

Water is my eye
Most faithful mirror
Fearless on my breath
Teardrop on the fire
Of a confession

This is the night of delirium. In this dreamlike room, we picture scenes of introspective feelings, illuminated by the fire of passion.

A fire that burns, questioning the very beat of the song.

The water-based mirror has nothing to say. It reflects the woman's face deep in confession, in a melody which is dark and enlightening at the same time. It is a melody which us able to reach our most mysterious depths and bring our feelings to light.

Night, night of matter
Black flowers blossom

Elisabeth Fraser, in her distinctive Scottish voice, echoes the sensations produced by this room of solemn riddles. She backs up the rhythmic syncope that marks the time. And this is **the**

time when Massive Attack have questions for us.

Then the room fades out over the sound of the last notes. The prayer announces the end of the delirium, the physical exhaustion that defines the end of the prophecy.

The time of riddles is over; the myth of *Teardrop* has fulfilled itself.

The echo of love is inside our chest, in the beat of our breath.

Lyrics

Love, love is a verb
Love is a doing word
Fearless on my breath

Gentle impulsion
Shakes me, makes me lighter
Fearless on my breath

Teardrop on the fire
Fearless on my breath

Night, night of matter
Black flowers blossom
Fearless on my breath

Black flowers blossom
Fearless on my breath

Teardrop on the fire
Fearless on my

Water is my eye
Most faithful mirror
Fearless on my breath

Teardrop on the fire
Of a confession
Fearless on my breath

Most faithful mirror
Fearless on my breath

Teardrop on the fire
Fearless on my breath

It's tumbling down (as in love falling apart)
It's tumbling down (as in love falling apart)

Love Will Tear Us Apart: The story of Joy Division's singular hit

By Carlo Affatigato

When Tony Wilson gave Ian Curtis a collection of Frank Sinatra records in 1980, he probably had no great expectations about the result, and he certainly felt that neither Ian nor the other band members would understand. Both Wilson and the producer Martin Hannett were of the opinion that Ian could draw inspiration from Sinatra, but they were also aware of the situation: Joy Division were **one of the brightest rising stars in the English post-punk scene**, their first album *Unknown Pleasures* having been a huge success, and their dark and depressed mood finding its way into the hearts of a generation of teenagers. Within the band, nobody in their right mind was thinking of writing Frank Sinatra-like songs. For the record, Ian Curtis was just 23 and, as the bassist Peter Hook explained more recently, a passion for Frank Sinatra doesn't come at that stage in life. You need to get older first.

Ian Curtis was not the kind of artist who prepared in the studio with hours of work and a very precise direction in mind. What he usually did was write the lyrics whenever he felt inspired, filling his notebooks with thoughts and sentences as they popped into his mind. In Joy Division, **Ian Curtis wasn't responsible for writing the songs: he was the one that perceived music before the others**, while the band members tried this or that tune, approaching them as soon as he felt that something good was coming out, then helping them to evolve this intuition into something bigger. When the melody was mature enough, he would reach for his diaries, grumbling about this or that phrase, selecting a couple of suitable lyrics and adapting them to fit the song. A minute later, the song would be over. And it wouldn't even have been recorded; it would still exist only in Joy Division's heads.

That was how it happened for *Love Will Tear Us Apart*: the first melodic intuition came from Peter Hook, Ian Curtis heard it and immediately started to lead the others, suggesting ideas for drums and guitars and then adding the lyrics. When the song came out in a more or less coherent form, Joy Division were a bit perplexed. The material was good, no doubt, but ... **where did that pop-like mood come from, with that growing chorus and that melody with clear nuances of optimism?** Joy Division were the apotheosis of dark wave, but now here it was, a "pop" song...

Why is the bedroom so cold
Turned away on your side?
Is my timing that flawed,
Our respect run so dry?
Yet there's still this appeal
That we've kept through our lives
Love, love will tear us apart
Again

Of course, the lyrics were anything but sunny. The love that would tear them apart was probably inspired by Ian Curtis' problematic marriage and his way of conceiving relationships, which irremediably ended up losing passion and devolving into resentment, accusations, tears and detachment. And, for a sensitive spirit, this easily led to despair: the kind that bites with sharp teeth, the kind that grabs you and leaves you with that ugly taste in your mouth. It is a taste of guilt, of an awareness that, if things didn't work, it's perhaps because you're not trying hard enough. Perhaps **because you are unable to. Or perhaps because you don't care anymore**.

Do you cry out in your sleep
All my failings expose?
Get a taste in my mouth
As desperation takes hold
Is it something so good
Just can't function no more?
When love, love will tear us apart
Again

That strange pop song might not fully convince Joy Division, but it sent Martin Hannett into a frenzy. At the time of recording, in March 1980, Hannett entered **a whirlwind of unprecedented perfectionism**. He saw in that song huge potential, and he had every intention of getting the best out of it. The refinement work lasted until late at night, to the point where the band members themselves, exhausted, began to leave the studio and go to sleep. But it wasn't done: Hannett called the drummer, Stephen Morris, at 4 am, because the beat needed to be reworked. For a long time, whenever Morris heard *Love Will Tear Us Apart*, he found himself wrenched back to that night again, his blood boiling with rage, remembering screaming at Hannett down the phone.

Eventually, *Love Will Tear Us Apart* came out as Hannett wanted it, with those tasty highs and lows in the voice of Ian Curtis, **that romantic passion between him and the microphone and the melody which is capable of elevating you to a new dimension**. Just like Frank Sinatra. And their unusual pop song also ended up pleasing Joy Division themselves, as they decided to shoot an amateur video clip that showed them during a practice session, at the T.J. Davidson Studios. At one point in that video, the images fade and the colours turn brown, but it seems intentional, a dark halo that hovers around Joy Division, even in their most charts-oriented song. These shots became the official video of the single and the song actually did its duty: it reached number one on the UK Indie Chart and earned respectable positions across the rest of the world. The road to preparation for the new album had just begun and they could smell another success. All they needed was another video and the plan for the perfect album would be completed.

But there wouldn't be any other videos. Ian Curtis took his own life three weeks after the shots of *Love Will Tear Us Apart*, when the single, the video, and the album hadn't even been officially released. The album, *Closer*, was released on July 18th, 1980, exactly two months after the death of the Joy Division leader, and it's universally recognised as his spiritual testament, the album where **he abandoned himself to the pain of living**. It describes his feelings in the rawest way possible, without limiting the effects.

On the day Joy Division were recording *Love Will Tear Us Apart*, U2 were present in the studio in order to meet Martin Hannett for the production of their first album. Bono later described that day in this way:

> *Talking to Ian Curtis was a strange experience. It was like two people inside of him. He's very warm, he talked very light and very well-mannered, very polite. But when he got behind the microphone he really surged forth; there was another energy. And Love Will Tear Us Apart was like him. As if there were two personalities, separate; there they were, torn apart.*

When the routine bites hard
And emotions won't grow
And were changing our ways
Taking different roads
Then love, love will tear us apart
Again

Lyrics

When routine bites hard
And ambitions are low
And resentment rides high
But emotions won't grow
And we're changing our ways
Taking different roads

Love, love will tear us apart again
Love, love will tear us apart again

Why is the bedroom so cold?
Turned away on your side
Is my timing that flawed?
Our respect run so dry?
Yet there's still this appeal
That we've kept through our lives

But love, love will tear us apart again
Love, love will tear us apart again

Do you cry out in your sleep?
All my failings exposed
Gets a taste in my mouth
As desperation takes hold
And it's something so good
Just can't function no more?

Love, love will tear us apart again
Love, love will tear us apart again

The Great Gig In The Sky: the story of Pink Floyd's beautiful gem

By Luca Divelti

"Chance is perhaps the pseudonym of God when he does not want to sign". You could write about and debate this famous quote from Nobel Prize winner Anatole France almost endlessly, finding so many examples of unexpected situations that often affect our lives.

Clare Torry probably didn't think twice when Pink Floyd called her in January 1973 to go to the Abbey Road Studios: for her it was a job like any other and, **although she was supposed to participate in the recording sessions of Pink Floyd's new album**, she wasn't in any way excited or hopeful. By that time, she had already lost hope that she would become a recognised singer in 60s England. Everybody had told her that her voice was respectable and that she didn't lack in any tone or skill, but the opportunity never came, seemingly continuously postponed by destiny. Or by chance.

While EMI was still suggesting that she recorded covers by other famous vocalists, the years had passed, and that aspiring singer-songwriter was now a woman who had placed her dreams in a drawer. Participating in the rock journeys of others was fine by her.

The track that she was supposed to sing on in was *The Great*

Gig in the Sky, which had originally been titled *The Mortality Sequence* or *The Religious Section*. The author was Rick Wright, and the song was initially based on a long solo on a Hammond organ, surrounded by voices singing about death. When he wrote it, Pink Floyd's keyboardist wanted to express **the sense of gradual passage from life to death**, with a characterisation of the piece in two distinct parts. The first showed the refusal to accept life's end, while the second was resignation and quiet acceptance.

But Pink Floyd were not entirely convinced. The song was missing something, and their sound engineer seemed to have identified the solution. **Alan Parsons persuaded them to introduce a female voice**, which could bring more evocative passages to the song.

Madeleine Bell and Doris Troy were initially suggested, but Parsons pushed for Clare Torry, who had impressed him in the past with her vocal talents. Unlike Bell and Troy, Clare was white and when she arrived to meet Pink Floyd, the band was not impressed. David Gilmour would confess afterwards that the young girl had looked more like a common English housewife than a singer.

Gilmour told her that there was no lyrics for *The Great Gig In The Sky*. She was supposed to **just sing as she thought about the passage from life to death**. It was basically improvising. Ultimately, Pink Floyd gave her complete freedom, but at the same time it was clear that they had no clear idea what they actually wanted her to do.

Torry was surprised by the unusual request, but she tried immediately to follow the band's guidelines. Her first performance was stopped almost immediately because she was singing *"Oh yeah."* **Pink Floyd had banned the lyrics**. The keyword was improvising, and she tried to jump in. But that required something more than a simple chorus singer: it needed somebody able to turn themselves into an instrument and merge their voice with Wright's sound.

On the second take, she tried to get into the song, but something was still wrong. She took a break and then tried for one last time. This time she decided not to follow the song: **she would just *be* the song**, imposing the emotional wave that moved inside her, letting go and really imagining the flow of life towards the inevitable end.

The sessions lasted three hours, then Torry left, not particularly convinced. She didn't think that her contribution had been appreciated by Alan Parsons and the band, and she was sure that they wouldn't choose her voice for *The Great Gig In The Sky*. For her performance, she received thirty pounds (twice the usual rate, since it was Sunday) and she returned to normal life.

Months later, she stumbled across a strange black album cover with a monolith in the middle and, intrigued, she picked it up and was surprised to read her name among the credits on *The Dark Side Of The Moon*. Her efforts had been rewarded.

Clare Torry's career didn't change, but her participation in one of the most famous records in music history allowed her to build a name. She was hired to sing jingles on advertisements and gained some popularity, both in the studio (Alan Parsons Project, Tangerine Dream, Culture Club, Roger Waters) and for live events.

Then the years passed and something changed within Torry; she was no longer happy to be known as the *"chorus singer on The Great Gig in the Sky"*. She wanted to seek a bit of acknowledgement after having being behind the scenes for so long. In 2004, she sued EMI and Pink Floyd, wanting to be recognised as a co-author of the song along with Rick Wright, rather than just a performer. She won the court case and, through an out-of-court agreement, she was refunded for the years during which her part on the record had not been truly recognised.

The dramatic and fascinating *The Great Gig In The Sky* would not have become such a world-renowned gem without Clare Torry's contribution. The emotional wave of those vocals, lying on the carpet of sound that was so meticulously put together by Richard Wright, really manage **to express the flow of existence and deliver a sense of passage between life and death**.

Who knows what would have happened, if Torry's name had never come to light: her voice wouldn't have entered into the history books, and perhaps Pink Floyd would have left *The Great Gig In The Sky* as an instrumental. It would have been a massive loss for everybody.

But luckily, this time, the pseudonym of God did want to sign.

Pearl Jam's Sirens: love is a fragile, human thing

By Diego Terzano

Among the classics of Pearl Jam's most recent history, *Sirens* sings of the urgency of reality. And it does it directly, creating a mutual, constant correspondence between music and words. ***Sirens* sings of fear; of things that fade before our very eyes**.

What cannot leave you indifferent is the depth nestled between the words. It's precisely this interweaving between those deep meanings and the ease with which you can listen to them, that marks the beauty of this song.

Have to take your hand, and feel your breath
For fear this someday will be over
I pull you close, so much to lose
Knowing that nothing lasts forever

The main characteristic of the lyrics is this dialectical conflict between the progressive degradation of reality and the need for stability, under a "simple" romantic context. It's the search for **an anchor that can save us from the swift passing of time**, and that can help us control our days. This fear is hidden within human relationships, specifically within love.

Nothing lasts, everything fades the moment it has occurred: the act of touching a lover's body, or holding their hand, is nothing but an attempt to escape death, to win over the void. Love is a fragile, human thing, but it's able to revitalise a fragile life, fighting the death that is always around us *("It's a fragile thing / This life we lead / [...] With death over our shoulders")*.

I didn't care before you were here,
I danced in laughter with the ever after
But all things change
Let this remain

There is no space for empty laughter, or for the ambitions of those who look towards the eternity without acknowledging the present or living within it. This blind dance to preserve love is therefore a ritual, a celebration of contacts and breaths:

Let me catch my breath and breathe
And reach across the bed
Just to know we're safe
I am a grateful man
The slightest bit of light
And I can see you clear

Of course the sirens are signs *("Hear the sirens / Covering distance in the night")*: they warn you about danger and tension, so the singer remains awake, prepared to face fear and the sounds of the city become warnings of the passing of time (*"The sound echoing closer"*). But and at the same time, they seem to come from somewhere else *("Will they come for me next time?")*. It's a persistent distraction from dialogue with a beloved one.

The enchantment, mixed with fear, then becomes an error; a journey weakened by the humanity we are all inescapably made of (*"For another choice, I have done / For any wrong choice I made / It is not part of my plans / Send you into the arms / Of another man"*). But, once again, it's within love that Eddie Vedder's voice finds its shelter. It's in the delicate balance of love that we can feel safe. The *"slightest bit of light"* in the darkness. And when we accustom our eyes to this darkness, we can finally see who we are looking for: *"I study your face / And the fear goes* *away".*

Recognising the shapes of one's beloved means, therefore, staying connected to life: **returning consistency and meaning to what has already been devoured by time**.

Lyrics

Hear the sirens, hear the sirens
Hear the sirens, hear the circus so profound
I hear the sirens more and more in this here town
Let me catch my breath to breathe
And reach across the bed

Just to know we're safe
I am a grateful man
The slightest bit of light
And I can see you clear
Have to take your hand, and feel your breath
For fear this someday will be over

I pull you close, so much to lose
Knowing that nothing lasts forever
I didn't care before you were here,
I danced in laughter with the ever after
But all things change
Let this remain
Hear the sirens covering distance in the night
The sound, echoing closer, will they come for me, next time?

For every choice, mistake I made, it's not my plan
To send you in the arms of another man
And if you choose to stay, I'll wait, I'll understand
It's a fragile thing, this life we lead,
If I think too much, I can't get over
Whelmed by the grace, by which we live
Our lives with death over our shoulders
Want you to know, that should I go,
I always loved you, held you high above, true
I study your face and the fear goes away

It's a fragile thing, this life we lead,
If I think too much, I can't get over
Whelmed by the grace, by which we live
Our lives with death over our shoulders
Want you to know, that should I go,
I always loved you, held you high above, true
I study your face and the fear goes away
I study your face and the fear goes away

Kashmir: Led Zeppelin, the desert, the mystic revelation

By Fabiana Falanga

Oh, let the sun beat down upon my face
And stars fill my dream
I'm a traveler of both time and space
To be where I have been
To sit with elders of the gentle race
This world has seldom seen
They talk of days for which they sit and wait
All will be revealed

Robert Plant once said, *"I wish we were remembered for Kashmir more than Stairway To Heaven"*. The song comes from the album *Physical Graffiti*, released in 1975.

Avoiding, as usual, commenting on any obscure meanings on *Stairway To Heaven*'s lyrics, he explains the dark period that gave birth to Kashmir, **almost like a mission that was there to be accomplished; a task to be completed**. This is reflected in the cohesive effect that this song had on the band, and in the power that made *Kashmir* the truest monument to Led Zeppelin.

It showcased their ability to project dreamlike visions, and to describe ethereal and poetic worlds.

All I see turns to brown
As the sun burns the ground
And my eyes fill with sand
As I scan this wasted land
Trying to find, trying to find
Where I've been

Kashmir is the place in which the band imagines **they are conversing with the old local prophets, about revelations and the coming of the Messiah**.

The sun burns, the sand dries their face.

Led Zeppelin are in a dreamlike delirium, in a mystical reality. The revelation will then become a prayer, an invocation, awaiting a direction.

And that's exactly what the guitar riff does. It is repeated endlessly, giving pace, and marking a path that also leads to mystical delusions, when the violins start to mock Robert Plant. As in the ancient iambic poem, the melody in the bridge seems to become playful, making fun of this delirium. At the same time, the violins hold the lyrics together: cutting, solemn, and visionary.

It's as if they are in a trance.

The voices echo mythological words.

Oh, pilot of the storm who leaves no trace
Like sorts inside a dream
Leave the path that led me to that place
Yellow desert stream
Like Shangri-la beneath the summer moon
I will return again
As the dust that floats finds you
We're moving through Kashmir

Kashmir is probably the song that best represents Led Zeppelin.

Kashmir is the power of hard rock.

Lyrics

Oh, let the sun beat down upon my face
And stars to fill my dream
I'm a traveler of both time and space
To be where I have been
To sit with elders of the gentle race
This world has seldom seen
They talk of days for which they sit and wait
All will be revealed

Talk in song from tongues of lilting grace
Sounds caress my ear
And not a word I heard could I relate
The story was quite clear

Oh, oh
Oh, oh

Oh, oh baby, I been flying
No yeah, mama, there ain't no denying
Oh, oh yeah I've been flying
Mama, mama, ain't no denying, no denying

All I see turns to brown
As the sun burns the ground
And my eyes fill with sand
As I scan this wasted land
Trying to find, trying to find, where I've been

Oh, pilot of the storm who leaves no trace
Like thoughts inside a dream
Heed the path that led me to that place
Yellow desert stream
Like Shangri-la beneath the summer moon
I will return again
Sure as the dust that floats high in June
When moving through Kashmir

Oh, father of the four winds fill my sails
Across the sea of years
With no provision but an open face
Along the straits of fear

Oh, oh
Oh, oh

Oh, when I'm on, when I'm on my way, yeah
When I see, when I see the way, you stay yeah

Oh, yeah-yeah, oh, yeah-yeah, when I'm down
Oh, yeah-yeah, oh, yeah-yeah, but I'm down, so down
Oh, my baby, oh, my baby, let me take you there
Come on, come on, oh, let me take you there, let me take you there

U2's One: the end of the crisis

By Ilaria Arghenini

Is it getting better?

When Bono wrote these words, it was 1991. He has no, U2 are going to break up. **Things are not getting better at all**.

The group experienced huge success at the end of the 80s and they were now at a critical point, in the Hansa Studios in Berlin, hoping that inspiration would somehow arrive.

He was very disappointed because U2 was the project in which he had invested all his plans, his future, just like the other members of the band, and sadly it looked like it was going to end up as another example of a short-lived musical project.

But the miracle happened one afternoon, in the form of **a melody that arrived by chance, played nervously with strings and instruments** in what looked like another unproductive afternoon in the studio.

"Suddenly something very powerful was happening in the room," Edge said. *"Everyone recognised it was a special piece."* The boys looked at each other; this was something new. Music and words slowly flew there, just when everything was almost gone.

Is it getting better
Or do you feel the same?
Will it make it easier on you now?
You got someone to blame
You say one love, one life (One life)
It's one need in the night
One love (one love), get to share it
Leaves you darling, if you don't care for it

It's the story of a break-up. A common routine that needs to be broken, because we are suddenly different. *One*'s lyrics are animated by that feeling of inevitable separation that all the members of U2 felt was coming.

Did I disappoint you?
Or leave a bad taste in your mouth?
You act like you never had love
And you want me to go without
Well it's too late, tonight
To drag the past out into the light

We started this together. We planned our future together, then we realised that we were not destined to stay together. Was there anything about me that you didn't like anymore?

A little anger also emerges because, hidden in the form of a question, there is the thought of the writer, who feels he has given a lot and not received as much. And at the same time, he recognises that getting lost in memories is useless: it doesn't help you to start over again.

Have you come here for forgiveness?
Have you come to raise the dead?
Have you come here to play Jesus?

Well, did I ask too much, more than a lot?

This question is the heart of the song. **Can we dare to ask to be happy?** If, until this point, the tone of the lyrics was still rational and analytical, then here the anger and the disappointment start to appear. You feel that they can be weapons with which one can accuse another, but the reality is that you cannot find the words. Destiny wins over you.

There is no one to blame, nothing that can be fixed: you are not angry because of something specific; you are just dissatisfied by a long-term plan that has been lost.

You gave me nothing, now it's all I got
We're one, but we're not the same
See we hurt each other, then we do it again
You say love is a temple, love is a higher law
Love is a temple, love is a higher law
You ask me of me to enter, but then you make me crawl
And I can't keep holding on to what you got
'cause all you got is hurt

The last section lights up these hopes: perhaps from this new situation we can start again, in a different way, forgetting our old plans. Perhaps we can re-emerge from this collapsed house of cards and build something new.

One love
One blood
One life
You got to do what you should
One life
With each other
Sisters and my brothers
One life
But we're not the same

We get to carry each other

U2 started over again from this song and resumed an adventure that still continues today. They were a step away from their final separation **but it was there that they realised that they had to stay together**; they were still able to create something beautiful again.

Sony ranked *One* fifth among the most popular songs of all time. The song has been the subject of covers by Johnny Cash and Joe Cocker.

The version with Mary J. Blige, released in 2006, was a huge success, becoming one of the best-selling songs for both Blige and U2, managing to overcome even the success of the original.

One would go on to become the main single from *Achtung Baby*. According to a survey conducted by the VH1, it's **the British song with the best lyrics ever**.

Lyrics

Is it getting better
Or do you feel the same?
Will it make it easier on you now?
You got someone to blame

You say one love, one life (One life)
It's one need in the night
One love (one love), get to share it
Leaves you darling, if you don't care for it

Did I disappoint you?
Or leave a bad taste in your mouth?
You act like you never had love
And you want me to go without

Well it's too late, tonight
To drag the past out into the light
We're one, but we're not the same
We get to carry each other
Carry each other

One, one

Have you come here for forgiveness?
Have you come to raise the dead?
Have you come here to play Jesus?
To the lepers in your head
Well, did I ask too much, more than a lot?
You gave me nothing, now it's all I got
We're one, but we're not the same
See we hurt each other, then we do it again
You say love is a temple, love is a higher law
Love is a temple, love is a higher law
You ask me of me to enter, but then you make me crawl

And I can't keep holding on to what you got
'cause all you got is hurt

One love
One blood
One life
You got to do what you should
One life
With each other
Sisters and my brothers
One life
But we're not the same
We get to carry each other
Carry each other

One, one

One love, one life

The Doors' Break On Through: the visionary poetics of Jim Morrison

By Dario Giardi

> *"If the doors of perception were cleansed, everything would appear to man as it truly is, infinite."*
>
> *William Blake*

Crossing the prophetic "doors of perception", as predicted by William Blake, was becoming the only way to escape from this dirty, corrupt, agonising world. At least, this was possible with our minds.

The desire to escape from reality hides a deep need to know. We are fascinated by the unknown and we keep asking ourselves questions like, "What is the meaning of life?" "What comes after death?" "Are we alone in the universe?"

The thing we all are most hungry for is knowledge. It's knowing what the meaning of life is, and it's precisely what science has never been able to provide. Only religion has been able to partly fill this void. And we all continue to seek a "sense" of our existence.

This doesn't mean that this sense must necessarily be a truth. We can imagine it, but nothing can extinguish the hidden desire that all of us have: we want to turn on the light in the dark room where dreams, hopes and truths become muddled.

You know the day destroys the night
Night divides the day
Tried to run
Tried to hide

Break on through to the other side

That's why *Break On Through,* the song that summarises Morrison's visionary poetics in the best possible way, **is an exhortation, an imperative: open the passage to the other side**.

The world is the kingdom of illusions and contraries *("You know the day destroys the night / Night divides the day")*, the place that tries to stop our research. Love, above all, can become a distracting refuge, the chain that imprisons the present. As Jim Morrison sings:

I found an island in your arms
Country in your eyes
Arms that chain
Eyes that lie

Break on through to the other side

Break on Through, found on The Doors' eponymous first album, exasperates us while summarising the origins of Morrison's entire poetry. Few verses give off an overall sense of alienated impotence in the same way, where **we and the author are imprisoned, crushed between reality and imagination**, between everyday life and visions. What we need is clear: we have to open up the pathway and reach the other side. **The side of "life" where you see things as they really are**.

Made the scene
Week to week
Day to day
Hour to hour
The gate is strait
Deep and wide

The "scene" is often understood as life, and the passage through the "strait gate" is a reference to Strait Is the Gate, André Gide's book about the complexities and terrors related to adolescence and the road to maturity. The opening the passage is therefore a process of growth, but it also represents awareness of the duality of life, and about the deceptions that it subjects us to. Your eyes offer you whole nations, but they are lying.

The answers that Jim Morrison gives are therefore uncertain and enigmatic. There is probably no way to achieve certainty when we ask questions of that magnitude. What is certain, however, is that one cannot help but **continue to seek balance amid so much chaos**, otherwise living will always be like being carried away on an unstoppable tide.

We chased our pleasures here
Dug our treasures there
But can't you still recall
The time we cried

Lyrics

You know the day destroys the night
Night divides the day
Tried to run
Tried to hide

Break on through to the other side
Break on through to the other side
Break on through to the other side

We chased our pleasures here
Dug our treasures there
But can you still recall
The time we cried

Break on through to the other side
Break on through to the other side

Everybody loves my baby
Everybody loves my baby
She gets high
She gets high
She gets high, yeah

I found an island in your arms
Country in your eyes
Arms that chained us
Eyes that lied

Break on through to the other side
Break on through to the other side

Break on through, oh, oh yeah

Made the scene
Week to week
Day to day
Hour to hour
The gate is strait
Deep and wide

Break on through to the other side
Break on through to the other side
Break on through
Break on through

You'll Follow Me Down: Skunk Anansie's cry of pain

By Fabiana Falanga

Going down.

Rising up.

Survived

Tonight

Still breathing heavily.

You'll Follow Me Down is the third single from the album *Post Orgasmic Chill,* released by Skunk Anansie in 1999.

In this song, Skin is the wind, strong and big, a priestess and narrator with a vital impact on the song.

As you watch me crawl

You stand for more

It happens, sometimes in life, that you get hurt. It happens that you want to punish yourself in the wrong way, and that you are unable to forgive yourself. It happens sometimes in life and in love. And sometimes it happens to drag those who love each other down into their own prison.

You do so much harm as two. You consume yourselves, and

the more you do it, the more you punish yourself, the more you indulge in this masochistic game of self-destruction, looking for a way to delegitimise yourself.

You are in a tunnel without forgiveness, a tunnel without excuses. A tunnel of solitude.

I don't want you, to forgive me,
You'll follow me down

It's the lament, the desperate scream of Skin. She already knows how it will end; she knows very well the game of both parties in this massacre, **when you can't see the end of the tunnel and you can only scream pain from deep within your throat**. And then, somehow, the exit is there, before you.

When you are one in another's arms, it's hard to tell what the rules are, or what the meaning of sin is. You forget what you were and what you've become, whether something brought you to this point or if you arrived by ourselves in this spiral of pain. If you are that way interminably, or whether one party has transformed the other.

And you're panic-stricken
Blood will thicken up
Tonight

And silence will tear you apart.

Fear: this old lady who loves to make fun of brilliant minds, who wants to decrypt the codes of the most profound intellects, **the puppet master of a theatre, manipulated by her wise claws**. She knows perfectly how to bring these hypnotised actors into the dangerous path of irrationality.

I don't want you to forgive me. First, I have to forgive myself.

That's what will happen after Skin's scream of pain, like a wounded beast, roaring and then rising up.

That's how you win your battle.

As your emotions fool you, (my) strong will rule

I won't feel restraint, watching you close sense down
I can't compensate, that's more than I've got to give

Lyrics

Survived, tonight
I may be going down,
'Cause everything goes round too,
Tight, tonight,
And it, you watch him crawl, you stand for more

And your panic stricken, blood will thicken up, tonight
'Cause I don't want you, to forgive me
You'll follow me down
You'll follow me down
You'll follow me down

Survive tonight
(I see your) head's exposed
So we shall kill, constructive might, s'right,
As your emotions fool you, (my) strong will rule

And your panic stricken, blood will thicken up, tonight
'Cause I don't want you, to forgive me
You'll follow me down
You'll follow me down
You'll follow me down

I won't feel restraint, watching you close sense down
I can't compensate, that's more than I've got to give

Yesterday: the secret story of The Beatles' perfect pop song

By Luca Divelti

"It's not possible that I'm the first one writing it: are you really sure that this melody is totally new?"

Paul McCartney was unsettled. He kept asking his companions whether this song, which had awoken him and forced him to the piano in the middle of the night, was really his creation and not someone else's work: yet *Yesterday* and his magical harmony had indeed never been written before.

McCartney was worried for one simple reason: **the notes had flown out of his unconscious mind so easily**, without any obstacles, that he had written a complete, finished version in just a few minutes. Only the lyrics were missing. He put it temporarily on hold, jotting down a few, meaningless words, waiting for more inspiration. That's how the first funny words of *Yesterday* came to be: *"Scrambled Eggs / oh my baby how I love your legs."*

Yesterday
All my troubles seemed so far away
Now it looks as though they're here to stay
Oh, I believe in yesterday

George Martin later said that the song had been composed

by McCartney in January 1964, but it was a year and a half later when the Liverpool Quartet recorded it for *Help!* What was initially presented to The Beatles' original producer as *Scrambled Eggs* took a few months to become *Yesterday,* while **McCartney was still not sure of what to do with it**. In December 1964, he played the song in front of The Yardbirds, hoping that the band would be interested in recording it. Eric Clapton's group declined, claiming that their rock imprinting didn't fit well with a ballad (who knows, though, how *Yesterday* would have sounded, played by Slow-Hand).

From that moment onwards, McCartney didn't miss an opportunity to play the song to friends, trying to clarify his doubts about the originality of the song. He even sat at the piano during the shooting of the *Help!* movie and let played it often, leading the exhausted director Richard Lester to threaten him with seizing the piano if he didn't stop.

Why she had to go I don't know, she wouldn't say
I said something wrong, now I long for yesterday

After a trip to Portugal in June 1965, where he finally made up his mind about recording the song, McCartney presented the definitive lyrics to his bandmates. **He was opposed to the use of violins, terrified by the excessive pomposity that they could bring**. He clashed with Martin, who eventually allowed him to direct the quartet as a way of convincing him to relent.

Paul McCartney (who recorded it practically solo, with no help from the other Beatles) agreed and *Yesterday* came to light as the first pop song with violins, which only contributed to the beauty of the melody.

Suddenly
I'm not half the man I used to be
There's a shadow hanging over me
Oh, yesterday came suddenly

The Beatles' perfect pop song, **the most played and recorded song in history** (with more than 2500 versions over time) pushed The Beatles beyond their usual musical boundaries and allowed them to learn from classical sounds, something that they would explore more later on. In 1980, McCartney described the song as his best and happiest composition, especially for his instinctive and mysterious birth, confessing to still being shocked about how it had arrived to him in a dream on a winter night.

Among the many occasions that the art world has celebrated the brilliance of *Yesterday*, the most touching and most impressive in living memory is probably from Sergio Leone's *Once Upon A Time In America*, and the ambitious soundtrack composed by the legendary Ennio Morricone. *Yesterday* becomes a touching tear that accompanies the protagonist in his old age, when he is still trying to find the answers to the events that marked his past life. There is perhaps no more exciting moment in the history of modern cinema than seeing Robert De Niro distraught, aged, with sunken eyes and apathetic movements, retracing the critical steps in his life that he would have liked to forget.

Yesterday
Love was such an easy game to play
Now I need a place to hide away
Oh, I believe in yesterday

Lyrics

Yesterday
All my troubles seemed so far away
Now it looks as though they're here to stay
Oh, I believe in yesterday

Suddenly
I'm not half the man I used to be
There's a shadow hanging over me
Oh, yesterday came suddenly

Why she had to go, I don't know
She wouldn't say
I said something wrong
Now I long for yesterday

Yesterday
Love was such an easy game to play
Now I need a place to hide away
Oh, I believe in yesterday

Why she had to go, I don't know
She wouldn't say
I said something wrong
Now I long for yesterday

Yesterday
Love was such an easy game to play
Now I need a place to hide away
Oh, I believe in yesterday

Daydreaming: Thom Yorke's life, nature, universe

By Dario Giardi

Let's not beat around the bush: *Daydreaming,* from Radiohead's album *A Moon Shaped Pool,* is a masterpiece, full of deep and surprising meanings.

The song is accompanied by a symbolic, poetic video. The protagonist is Radiohead's lead singer, Thom Yorke. We see him emerging from an intense light that symbolises the place where souls remain. From there, from that initial state of bliss, **each of us walks towards a state of being and faces an earthly path**.

This goes
Beyond me
Beyond you

Once there, Yorke opens the doors to see what kind of life is waiting for him, what kind of life he chose. He walks once again through **the salient moments of his childhood**, the hospital that will mark his first years. As a child, Thom Yorke was subjected to various surgeries to correct a congenital paralysis of the left eye. In the first five years of his life, he went through many operations, which would cause partial blindness and a problem with his left eyelid - the same feature that would one day become his unmistakable somatic trait.

We see different places, different houses, reminding us that the Yorke family never establishes itself in a place for long; something that has created some difficulties with forming new friendships, thus creating an atmosphere of isolation and solitude around Yorke.

You often encounter doors with "Exit" written above, but in his music, we see Yorke take the opposite way every time. **He wants to go on, he wants to see, even if certain visions can hurt**.

We are

Just happy to serve

Just happy to serve

You

Then we have some scenes of daily life, people in the laundry, people eating, or at the beach. Then an empty house, a sign of the separation with his wife Rachel Owen, the companion of a lifetime. It was **a painful separation that would mark him deeply**, something that emerges when you listen carefully to the most recent album. In an emblematic scene, we see a teenager slamming the door on Yorke, as he passes through a hallway. It is a moment that symbolises and recalls his children, who will become more distant towards him after the separation.

Then, suddenly, natural images come into view and elevate the soul to a higher stage of consciousness, recalling the place where everything began, from where the protagonist's soul took his the first steps. **It's only in nature that we can all find serenity and peace**.

The white room

By a window

Where the sun comes through

The verses represent the deep human desire to live immersed and in symbiosis with nature. **It is a nature, however, that not even dreamers can protect now**, as Thom seems to warn us. His message arrives very directly to us:

pollution, climate change, the melting of the polar icecaps. The damage is done.

Dreamers
They never learn
Beyond the point
Of no return
And it's too late
The damage is done

Then, at last, he falls asleep next to the fire. He saw what life is waiting for him and he acepted it with a smile, because ultimately, **every life is chosen by us and it's there to be lived**, along with all the challenges we are supposed to face.

Lyrics

Dreamers
They never learn
They never learn
Beyond, beyond the point
Of no return
Of no return

And it's too late
The damage is done
The damage is done

This goes
Beyond me
Beyond you

The white room
By a window
Where the sun comes
Through

We are
Just happy to serve
Just happy to serve
You

Portishead's Roads: the introspection in front of life's crossroads

By Fabiana Falanga

There is a moment in life when we see clearly all the arteries that the body of life is made of: millions of roads, millions of wasted opportunities, compromises and choices, victories and bets.

This is life, branching off in countless directions, driven forward by a river of energy that never stops. **Once you choose your road, you have to deal with its twists and turns**.

Then, there is a second moment in life when you realise that you are alone in this choice. **You reach a crossroads with your life's baggage accompanying you**; your failures and gratifications, your unexplained or rational circumstances, your expectations and certainties.

Frozen to myself

I got nobody on my side

And surely that ain't right

What happened before that moment doesn't matter anymore. No one can see it. **You are alone, both a rival and ally to yourself, a victim and executioner of wrong choices**, the benefactor and beneficiary of your own success.

Oh, can't anybody see
We've got a war to fight
Never found our way
Regardless of what they say

Roads is Portishead's best trip hop number from their first album *Dummy*. The prayer of Beth Gibbons, who delicately balances her vocals atop a storm of bass and reverberation that resembles a flashbacks, with sound distortions that float like bubbles in a calm sea.

Storm, in the morning light
I feel
No more can I say
Frozen to myself

Frozen, petrified, the singer tells us of **the awareness of her inevitable and necessary solitude**, and that loneliness that soon or later arrives in the life of everyone. It's a sign of growth, not just a condition. It's the moment when you choose your road, and let it become your own.

The song is Gibbons' battle cry. The moment when she recognises that she is alone and she's ready to go on and become invincible, for herself and for others.

This is the moment in life when she discovers her road.

How can it feel, this wrong
From this moment
How can it feel, this wrong

Lyrics

Oh, can't anybody see
We've got a war to fight
Never found our way
Regardless of what they say

How can it feel, this wrong
From this moment
How can it feel, this wrong

Storm, in the morning light
I feel
No more can I say
Frozen to myself
I got nobody on my side
And surely that ain't right
And surely that ain't right

Oh, can't anybody see
We've got a war to fight
Never found our way
Regardless of what they say

How can it feel, this wrong
From this moment
How can it feel, this wrong
How can it feel, this wrong
This moment
How can it feel, this wrong

Oh, can't anybody see
We've got a war to fight
Never found our way
Regardless of what they say

How can it feel, this wrong
From this moment
How can it feel, this wrong

Zombie: The Cranberries' Anti-Violence Anthem

By Luca Divelti

Northern Ireland was an ever-present in the chronicles of the last century, a period where violence raged in the streets and clashes between Protestants and Catholics saw civilians living in fear of being in the wrong place at the wrong time.

On March 20th, 1993, Tim Parry and Jonathan Ball, three and twelve years old respectively, were killed by a bomb placed by IRA in Warrington, Northern England, and dozens of other people were injured in the explosion. The bloodbath and the involvement of two children shook the minds of British citizens, **who once again had to count the innocent victims of a seemingly endless clash**.

Dolores O'Riordan was among them.

Another head hangs lowly
Child is slowly taken
And the violence caused such silence
Who are we mistaking?

The voice of The Cranberries, at that time engaged in a tour in England, was shocked and **the emotion of the moment inspired her to grab her guitar and write some verses**, without thinking about how difficult such a topic could be. This was the birth of *Zombie*, one of the definitive 90s rock anthems and the best-known of the Irish group.

Other artists before her had addressed the Northern Ireland issue and its tragic events (among others John Lennon, Paul McCartney, U2, Simple Minds and The Police), focusing mainly on the infamous events of Bloody Sunday, which in 1973 represented the peak of the violence between the various factions involved in the conflict. *Zombie* became O'Riordan's protest song **against a situation that was already out of control**. The shock forced her to go beyond the opposition between Protestants and Catholics, focusing on the death of two innocent children.

With their tanks and their bombs
And their bombs and their guns
In your head in your head they are crying

Released in September 1994 (a couple of weeks after the historic ceasefire) on *No Need To Argue*, *Zombie* raised the status of The Cranberries beyond any predictions, thanks also to the video, which was directed by Samuel Bayer (Nirvana, Blind Melon). The videoclip showed glimpses of life on the streets of Northern Ireland, mixing little boys, passers-by and soldiers with The Cranberries overlapping in the images. The moment when **O'Riordan, covered with gold, appeared under a cross at the children's side** (to remember Tim and Jonathan) catapulted the video to fame, securing its place as one of the most iconic of all time.

This protest song is an aggressive and angry response to the passive acceptance of what was happening by part of the Irish population, which at some point had started to become accustomed to the indifference, just like the lifeless beings mentioned in the song title. The Northern Ireland conflict would begin the long and difficult path towards peace in 1998 and the two main promoters, John Hume and David Trimble, would win the prestigious Nobel Peace Prize that year. **The band playing at the award ceremony? The Cranberries.**

Dolores O'Riordan died on January 15th, 2018, but the oxygen from her most famous song hasn't yet stopped fuelling the flames of modern music.

What's in your head?
In your head
Zombie, zombie, zombie

Lyrics

Another head hangs lowly
Child is slowly taken
And the violence, caused such silence
Who are we mistaken?

But you see, it's not me
It's not my family
In your head, in your head
They are fighting
With their tanks, and their bombs
And their bombs, and their guns
In your head, in your head
They are crying

In your head
In your head
Zombie, zombie, zombie

What's in your head
In your head
Zombie, zombie, zombie

Another mother's breaking
Heart is taking over
When the violence causes silence
We must be mistaken

It's the same old theme
Since nineteen-sixteen
In your head, in your head
They're still fighting
With their tanks, and their bombs
And their bombs, and their guns

In your head, in your head
They are dying

In your head
In your head
Zombie, zombie, zombie
What's in your head
In your head
Zombie, zombie, zombie

Index